Gravity and Grace

OTHER LUTHERAN VOICES TITLES

See www.lutheranvoices.com

Gravity and Grace
Reflections and Provocations

Joseph Sittler

Foreword by Martin E. Marty

Augsburg Fortress
Minneapolis

GRAVITY AND GRACE
Reflections and Provocations

Large-quantity purchases or custom editions of these books are available at a discount from the publisher. For more information, contact the sales department at Augsburg Fortress, Publishers, 1-800-328-4648, or write to: Sales Director, Augsburg Fortress, Publishers, P.O. Box 1209, Minneapolis, MN 55440-1209.

Scripture quotations unless otherwise noted are from the Revised Standard Version of the Bible, copyright 1946, 1952, and 1971 by the Division of Christian Education of the National Council of Churches.

Chapter 6, "Moral Discourse in a Nuclear Age," is reprinted from the March 6, 1985 issue of *The Christian Century,* copyright 1985 Christian Century Foundation. Used by permission.

Chapter 7, "Aging: A Summing Up and a Letting Go," is reprinted from Volume 2, Number 4 of *Health & Medicine,* the Journal of the Health and Medicine Policy Research Group. Used by permission.

Editor: Thomas S. Hanson

Cover design: Koechel Peterson and Associates, Inc., Minneapolis, Minn.
www.koechelpeterson.com

ISBN 0-8066-5173-3

The paper used in this publication meets the minimum requirements of American National Standard for Information Sciences—Permanence of Paper for Printed Library Materials, ANSI Z329.48-1984. ⊛ ™

Manufactured in the U.S.A.

09   08   07   06   05   1   2   3   4   5   6   7   8   9   10

This book, *Gravity and Grace,* was first published by Augsburg Publishing House in 1986. It was brought to life by Paul A. Hanson and Shirley Teig of the American Lutheran Church Division for Life and Mission in the Congregation and Linda-Marie Delloff, then managing editor of *The Christian Century.* Together they selected and edited excerpts from numerous lectures, papers, and conversations with Joseph Sittler.

Through this collection of "reflections and provocations," many who had been Sittler's students and the thousands of those who had not, were challenged and prodded to expand their own vision of God and grace by this graceful thinker and speaker.

This edition contains most of the original book, though chapters 6-9 (and some individual reflections) have been omitted for reasons of space limitations. Questions for individual reflection and group discussion have been added at the end of each chapter.

The intent with this edition of *Gravity and Grace* is to introduce Joseph Sittler's voice to a new generation of Christians and to reacquaint those of an older generation for whom Sittler was a significant influence in the theology, practice, and vision of their faith.

Thomas S. Hanson, editor
2004

Contents

Foreword

From the original foreword by Martin E. Marty

The publisher and editor (Linda-Marie Delloff), but not the author, have asked me to introduce Joseph Sittler to new readers and to suggest to his devotees how to read this book. The author made no such request because (a) he sees no reason to make a fuss, and (b) if you asked him how to read it, he would say something like, "Well, you take it off the shelf. You open it. You use your eyes, proceeding from the upper left-hand corner to the lower right, line by line. Then you turn the page. . . ." Why should one need lessons in reading that rare theological work that is rare because it is so clear, so intelligible? Yet a book like this does merit a foreword, and those in charge asked me, and I enjoy the responsibility of passing it on with a few words.

First, recall that we imagined Sittler saying, "You use your eyes. . . ." On these pages the theologian lets slip what is a consuming complication of his life but for which he asks no pity: much of his eyesight (though none of his "vision") is gone. For many of us he remains not only (in age) our sage, but (almost sightless) our seer. Yet he has had to accommodate with difficulty—and, I imagine and hope, not total grace—to the progressive loss of eyesight. And what use he made of those eyes! At a University of Chicago Divinity School luncheon where he addressed us as an emeritus, the host asked for questions. Students, who confide in Sittler as a senior pastor in their midst when they are one-on-one, were diffident, so the host turned to me. "Joe, if you had your full sight back for just one afternoon, what would you go to see?" I had not even reached the oral question mark when he shot back, "Chartres." Then he gave us a five-minute lecture on the glories of the blues in the cathedral windows there.

This book, excerpts from Sittler's numerous lectures, papers, and conversations, can be read chunk by chunk, paragraph by paragraph. The model is something like the Penseés of Pascal, or aphoristic writing in general. Modern literary critics and language philosophers like to debate what is the unit of discourse: the word, the sentence, the paragraph, the book, the life work? Sittler caresses his words and has devoured poetry in order to get words right. When people speak of his eloquence, they repeat various sentences which are natural-born epigraphs and aphorisms. Yet his prime unit is the paragraph. Each one has space and time for a triggering incident on which he reflects, a rehearsal of the reasons why he brings it up, and the reflection. Watch for examples.

Second, a how-to-read-Sittler manual has to say that he considers nothing he writes or says to be a finished product. The God of these pages is a God honored by humble traditions, but a God to be trusted—Sittler joins those who know not fully why—in regard to the future. Hans Urs von Balthazar has written that "resignation" may be a fine humanistic way of coping with physical decline, with aging, with life-toward-death, but it is not a particularly Christian virtue. Jesus, at least, embodies the forward look that we associate with youth and its adventure. Sittler, here as elsewhere, has spent too much energy reflecting on aging for us to dismiss his elegiac tone, his evocations of evening and autumn in life. Yet, however much he may protest youth cult and culture and refuse to see himself typed with it, there is something about his forward bent that should impel readers of these paragraphs to see him venturing to propose ways for their futures.

Someone asked Sittler what exactly he would counsel the church if it were to ask him how to go about reforming itself or being reformed. His ready answer was, "Watch your language!" This is a third element to pass on to new leaders. He did not mean, as parents used to mean, that we should not be profane or obscene or violent. "Watch your language" meant and means, "take care" with your speech and writing. Language, which for him helps define not only the human but the divine-human connection, demands and deserves great attention. I am sure Sittler would-be fussing and messing, seeking to get each line right. Yet despite his handicaps, he served the church by exemplifying what he counseled. He watched his language and wants us to do the same.

This book contains surprisingly sullen and almost angry passages. Usually they are directed at the careless, particularly if these have the care of souls and the privilege of communicating, against "flatulent" remarks by clerics, and stupid ministers who do not read (and thus they will never know they are being scolded here). At the same time, there is a constant respect for the Christian congregation. Yet ministers who read this have no reason to do so in a spirit of masochism. He honors their profession and helps them "watch" to improve it.

One is tempted to say "Watch for this!" and "Watch for that!" in the spirit of the underpaid and overeager tour guide. The sights along the way in this book do not need pointers-out or exclaimers. They take care of themselves. Watch, instead, for a sustained effort to build on a trust in God that Sittler cannot account for, but which is his delight. Get to know his parents and others who have influenced him.

Watch, under it all, for the man his seminary colleagues and students called The Old Brooder brooding about human limits, and the limitless bounty of God in nature and grace. Nature and grace: these are the themes that Sittler would bring together, after "men" in his own and other Christian churches had rent them asunder. Watch for the way he displays what he talks about: a natural affirmation in a fallen world, and a grace that never lets itself be confined. For Sittler, grace is not something that forces smiles or induces arm-waving "Praise the Lords," though he would smile and pray. His grace is known so plausibly because this graceful thinker and speaker has also measured what is grave about life, and about his life. And so this book is the Gravity and Grace of Joseph Sittler, and of Sittler's God.

Pass it on.

Martin E. Marty
1986

Preface

By its own title, *Gravity and Grace* leads us into the theological constructions of Joseph Sittler. Sittler's writings draw from two contexts. The first context in the title is our human grounding into the creation: Gravity. We are bound to the universe by more than the forces of science. According to Sittler we are bound to the universe through the creative power and intent of God. That idea moves us into the second part of the title: Grace. Sittler identifies the grace of God as the foundation of God's purpose and plan for the cosmos. Well titled, *Gravity and Grace* moves the reader through the constructions of Sittler's ideas as he addresses God's work in the universe, through the church and within the lives of individuals.

The first setting that Sittler draws from is the universe or, as Sittler would say, the cosmos. Gravity holding us to the earth demands that we see with Sittler the interrelatedness of all pieces of God's creation. Beginning in the creation story, Sittler's writings are grounded in the identification of a continuous record of God's participation in creation. This record begins with the Word in Genesis, it continues through the Incarnation of God in the Christ, moves outward through the life and teaching of Jesus and through the moment of death, into the resurrection and on to God's eternity. As we read Sittler, we are invited to see God's continuous grace-filled activity.

Speaking to the church, Sittler uncovers some of what it means to claim the identity of "Christian." The reader must first see life from the perspective of Sitter: The creation is the cradle of our existence. The church is one piece of the matrix, the interconnected human-creation relationship. Sittler invites us get our hands dirty, touching the flowers, animals, trees. When we retouch the creation we can relearn the compassion and love necessary to touch the most wounded among us.

Sittler approaches us as individuals to prod our minds lazy with theological satisfaction. The Word of God calls us into action empowered by grace. Sittler demands that we leave behind our complacency and work alongside the Christ in the task of redeeming our time from the evils that rise from human imagination.

Through Grace, the second context in this title, or because of it, Sittler's musings continue to challenge us. He demands that we know God's grace to be the foundation of all of God's interactions with the cosmos. Sittler recognizes that most of the world has a fuzzy understanding of the doctrine of grace. For Sittler, the grace of God has many facets. First, grace is the movement of the Spirit attending to humanity as a redemptive life. But grace is more than that. Grace is the fullness of God. In life, we experience God's grace through moments of innovation, spontaneity, and creativity.

Together Gravity and Grace set the boundaries for Sittler's call to faith: Trust all to God and risk everything. Sittler wrote that faith means to accept what God gives, knowing that God is the giver as well as the gift. Faith is not focused exclusively on Jesus. Narrowed and exclusive faith blinds us to the revelation that it is God, always God, who is acting this moment in and through the creation.

There are challenges in reading Sittler as the church lives in this twenty-first century. First, there are names, references, and events important to Sittler that are too far removed from our experience. A second challenge is that most of the work included here was written before a time of gender awareness. The lack of specific focus by Sittler does not indicate his participation in church attitudes that marginalized groups or individuals from the work of theology. Finally, the Lutheran community, the church that Sittler knew, continues to struggle and change. Sittler's thoughts transcend time as they call us into a life of grace and action.

Those who knew him are anxious to share with me their stories of Joe each time I have the opportunity to speak about his theology. This volume is the opportunity to enter into conversation again. This reissuing is for all of us whose copies of *Gravity and Grace* are in tatters on the shelf. It is also for those who have never heard of Sittler and yearn for an authentic voice. Immerse yourself in the images, the metaphors, the carefully chosen words of Sittler as he lays before us the grace of God found in the Word of God.

Elaine Siemsen
St. Olaf College
2004

1

Nature and Grace

Humankind has been here longer than my generation first supposed. Our history is yearly disclosed by research to be more and more complicated. But our existence on the earth as a small part of a single system of systems within systems that spin out into dreamlike magnitudes—this is the actual world of reflection in which the Christian faith must now ask after the relevance of its language. If we talk about creation, we mean more than the chrysanthemums and the bullfrogs and men and women. If we talk about redemption, we must ask if the ultimate meaning of redemption is confined to God's historical action for the human race in this place.

Theology is not only knowledge of human reflection about God; theology is also a constant doing, as well as a remembering, a transmitting, a refining. Theology is something that the church does, not only something that it has. Therefore a theologian is not simply a deep freeze in which the past is preserved and at certain times thawed out briefly for the attentive listener; theology is a vocation in which the accumulations of the past and the experiences of the present are always freshly attuned to the phenomena of the emerging, changing, frenetically racing world.

There are no logical, anthropological, psychological, or sociological definitions of homo sapiens in the Bible. But there are certain paradigms of where humanity stands. For example, in the very first chapter of the Old Testament there is a story in which human beings are spoken of from three angles of vision, as creatures with three dimensions, or as constituted by three enormous forces. First of all, we are from God. God is prior; he is the creator, we are the creatures.

God calls us into existence. As Calvin used to put it, "Man's existence is a subsistence." We subsist under God's eternal existence. So our God relationship is the first building block of this structure.

God made the first human not out of angelic substance or out of sheer gas or wind, but out of the dust of the earth. This is a symbolic and powerful way of saying that the human race belongs to the biological order. We are part of nature. We cannot lay aside our natural beginning, our rootedness in the same ecological system that characterizes the natural world. That is both a psychological report and a theological report.

The main point of the story of Eve is not that God made a woman, but that he made another human being. For a solitary person has not the possibility of becoming a person. The human relationship of one person to another, person to neighbor, is a determining factor of personhood. This aspect of relationship, then, is the second element of the human structure.

And the third building block is that God put his creatures in the garden. God places, thrusts, his creatures, roots them in nature. And the human relationship to nature is such that we are to tend it. The garden, the world of nature, is God's other creation, which stands alongside his creation of persons, not as neutral or mute, but as a living creation which has its own unique integrity and which defines the human place in the world.

Nature is never, for Jesus, simply a resource out of which we are to dig iron and copper and zinc, and pump oil; it is the theater of human life—the garden of our life—which it is our obligation to care for.

You can't solve the whole problem of nature's care by stewardship. That's a perfectly good word and a very powerful idea, but it's not a big enough doctrine; it's not central enough. For nothing less than the doctrine of grace would be an adequate doctrine to shape the Christian community's mind and practice in a way appropriate to the catastrophe in the environment.

God creates his creation in grace. The creation itself is a realm of grace.

We must read the text very carefully: "The heavens are telling the glory of God" (Ps. 19:1). But we must not go on to say that the heavens disclose the will of God. By going out on Sunday morning and looking up at the heavens from the seventh tee, one has not performed an adequate act of obedience. The will of God is not disclosed via the heavens—though the glory of God, according to the Scriptures, is.

Moralistic little essays here and there telling us to recycle the newspapers and smash the cans (and we should do both) are not sufficient efforts to care for our environment. There must be some primary theological reflection on this point.

What I am appealing for is an understanding of grace that has the magnitude of the doctrine of the Holy Trinity. The grace of God is not simply a holy hypodermic whereby my sins are forgiven. It is the whole giftedness of life, the wonder of life, which causes me to ask questions that transcend the moment.

I am interested in the reality or the presence of the grace of God in the creation, because only the doctrine of grace will be adequate to change the spirit of our minds whereby we deal with timber and oil, fish and animals, and the structure of cities, urban design, homes for people, places to work—all these mundane, concrete things that yet constitute the anchorage of our hearts, the home of our daily lives.

Nature is for enjoyment, in the profound meaning of enjoyment: to honor a thing for what it is, to consent to its being what it is and not another thing. Use nature, for sure, but use it only according to its inherent dignity.

Contemporary Humans

Contemporary humans are diminished because our roots are not as deep or as widely spread as were those of our forebears into the field, the forest, the woods. They do not touch the flowers, the animals, the daily tasks on the farm. Contemporary people, contemporary children particularly, think that hamburgers come from McDonalds. They think that Bordens makes milk and Kraft makes cheese. The closest any of them ever come to a lamb is a wool jacket. This increasing distance from the natural world has made our vocabulary bereft of natural images, has almost stripped us of the possibility to talk of ourselves in relation to God's creation.

In the course of history the human race has not only sailed the seas but has pierced beyond its earth homeland. Now it is piercing into the deepest recesses of molecular life and cellular life. We are constituted by our transactions with nature—not just the cattle on a thousand hills or the molecules under a thousand microscopes. So deeply are we formed by our experiences of nature that if the gospel is going to be addressed to contemporary human beings, it's got to have a God who follows those probings, a God of nature thus understood.

When We Turn

When we turn the attention of the church to a definition of the Christian relationship with the natural world, we are not stepping away from grave and proper theological ideas; we are stepping right into the middle of them. There is a deeply rooted, genuinely Christian motivation for attention to God's creation, despite the fact that many church people consider ecology to be a secular concern. "What does environmental preservation have to do with Jesus Christ and his church?" they ask. They could not be more shallow or more wrong.

Several years ago I attended three conferences relating to this topic. The first was at Massachusetts Institute of Technology, and it dealt with the obligation of the scientific community for the environment. Attending were physical chemists, cosmographers, astrophysicists, physicists, agricultural experts, and others. The conference was characterized by carefully written, data-rich, and responsible papers on all aspects of the environment—its present state, its fragility, what must be done to preserve the ecological structure of our world.

At the end of the six-day meeting, a press conference was called, and a small committee that had been assigned to prepare a summary statement came to a remarkable conclusion. They said, in substance, "There is much that the scientific community can do, and much more that we propose to do about the care of the environment. But no conceivable enhancement of research methodology, no conceivable addition of public funds, no cries of warning will make any considerable difference unless we are all changed in the spirit of our minds."

I doubt if they knew they were quoting St. Paul in that last phrase, which is extremely important. We must not just change our minds. Minds are very fragile things; we change them almost daily. But they said something much more profound: we must be changed "in the spirit of our minds." With our minds we look at things, but in the spirit of our minds we behold things. The difference here is not only linguistic. To look at a thing is what the psychologists call an act of perception. To behold a thing means to regard it in its particularity—its infinite preciousness, irreplaceability, and beauty. This statement stimulated my thoughts on the problem of humanity and the natural world.

Then I went to another conference, one held at the University of Chicago and attended by teachers of the country's leading law schools. The topic was: "What is the role of public law in the care and protection of the environment?" The lawyers presented serious papers, but I read a news release at the end of it, and it was uncannily like the one from the conference of scientists. They said there is much that public law ought to do, and will do, for the environment. No conceivable operation of public law by itself, however, will provide any significant solution to human misuse of the earth. In addition, they pointed out, the role of public law is important, but its pace is very slow. For there to be a law there must first be information. Then a consensus must be forged; then a law must be pushed through to legislation, and whereas the degradation of our environment is proceeding at a gallop, public law advances at a crawl.

The third conference I attended was by no means as prestigious as the first two. It wasn't really a conference, in fact; it was a meeting of some clergy on the same topic. During the meeting, a well-respected clergyman uttered this particularly foolish statement: "This is my Father's world, this is God's world. And if God wants us to take care of the world in a certain way, and we don't do it, then God will certainly, in his way, look after things no matter what we do." I thought that a very strange reading of the doctrine of God and the doctrine of nature. It reminded me of some wonderful passages in the Old Testament: "And God gave them what they wanted and made them sick of it," or, "God led them home by way of the wilderness." The reprisals of God's creation against its abuse may be slow and invisible for generations, but God is just. Sooner or later nature reacts against its exploitation.

In my own Lutheran tradition, the development of our theology, our hymnody, our liturgical language, our ordinary preaching almost never intersects the problems of the natural world. Why is that? This is, indeed, my Father's world. We sing the hymn, but we do not preach the substance, nor do we get it very often in our prayers or our liturgy. Why is that? This question has bothered me for a long time.

I think the reasons Lutheran theology and piety are not known for any specific or any analytically delicate feeling for the problems of the environment are several. First, we use the Old Testament in our praises and in our liturgical actions with right gratitude, but we have quite sharply misunderstood the first chapter of Genesis. "And God blessed them, and God said to them, 'Be fruitful and multiply, and fill the earth and subdue it; and have dominion over the fish of the sea and over the birds of the air and over every living thing that moves upon the earth'" (Gen. 1:28). The word *dominion* is a direct English effort to translate the Latin. In English, dominion suggests domination, but that is an incorrect translation. The Hebrew statement is, rather, "And God said you are to exercise care over the earth and hold it in its proper place."

When one looks at that statement and considers the identity of the people to whom it was addressed, it makes considerable sense. The ancient Hebrews were surrounded by Canaanites who were nature worshipers, and God said to his chosen, "Nature is God's, but it is not God. Nature is not to be worshiped, but it is my gift, and you are to exercise care for my gift. You are to hold it in its proper place, and its proper place is very high."

In that same chapter is a discussion of the Garden of Eden. There is the root of the fact that when men and women want to express something that is the very profundity of their spirits, they reach for an analogy from nature: "Now is the winter of our discontent/Made glorious summer by this sun of York," or, "My love is like a red red rose." Why do I have to use the language of nature to serve the expanded understanding of my personhood? Because my personhood is of nature, natural but enspirited by the breath of the Creator. We have not taken enough account of the nature images in the Bible.

The second reason our Lutheran understanding of this matter is inadequate is the perverse side of one of our greatest virtues: our radical Christocentrism. That is, our theology is almost exclusively a theology of the Second Article. "I believe in God the Father Almighty, maker of heaven and earth" (Article One). "And in Jesus Christ, His only Son, our Lord" (Article Two). "And in the Holy Spirit, the Lord and giver of life" (Article Three). These three are ways of speaking of the activity and reality of one God. But we Lutherans have had a compulsive fascination with the Second

Article. Jesus Christ, and him crucified, is the heart of Luther's, and hence our, theology.

In the Sixteenth Century

In the sixteenth century, fundamental tilts and accents and statements of our theological tradition were given classical formation. In that century's Reformation, what was needed as over against the human authoritarianism, the sacramentalism, the sacerdotalism, and the monasticism of the church was a radical Christocentric doctrine. And Luther was tactically right in putting forth the idea, "Unless I be shown that this is the gospel of Christ, I buy nothing else."

Luther was tactically quite right, and he was biblically quite right. But to be right at a certain moment is not necessarily to be completely adequate for all time. Luther is not always utterly adequate to every situation.

It is important that we understand our Christocentrism at the point, as it were, at which God becomes historically present, radiant, incandescent, available for our knowing and historical reality. This is the doctrine of God in Christ. God was in Christ reconciling the world unto himself—but it is always God, God, God, in all three persons.

Against this background we must understand the doctrine of grace. Each person in the Holy Trinity points to and accents the reality and the activity of the one God. So we cannot say love belongs to God and grace belongs to Jesus.

We talk about the Old Testament in the same way. We often talk as if the God of the Old Testament were a God of law only; but then we go right ahead in our liturgy and use the Psalms, which have a magnificent rhetoric of grace. In sermons we keep on talking about the Old Testament being all law, but God is always a God of grace. The Hebrew word translated *charis* or *grace* in the New Testament, is *hesed* or *hen,* and these two Hebrew words can only be translated to mean that one lives under a God of grace. David knew that and died in that faith. Abraham knew it, as St. Paul and the letter to the Hebrews both testify.

The manger child was the incarnation of grace, not the inventor or the origin of grace. Thus, if grace characterizes the whole of Christian theology—God the Father, God the Son, and God the Holy Spirit—what does this mean for our understanding of the natural world?

Christian motivation comes out of discipleship: understanding the will and the purpose of God. This reluctant literature that some of the denominations are issuing on stewardship is not wrong, but it isn't very exciting either. What we need is to relate back to the first point: the change in the spirit of our minds must come about by putting the grace of God behind the eyes with which we look at the world and into the hands with which we touch the world.

And of course God's grace inheres in nature too. The early church fathers of the third and fourth centuries used two wonderful phrases that have almost fallen out of contemporary theology. They talked about "special grace" and "common grace." By "special grace" they meant that historical, incomparable appearance of the grace of God in Jesus Christ. But Augustine said that we were all born into the world of "common grace." Common does not mean low or moderate; it means available to everyone. By common grace the early church thinkers meant the grace into which everyone is born.

Before one is baptized, or even if one never is, such grace meets one in God's creation. There is a common grace in the pear tree that blooms and blushes. There is common grace in the sea (that massive cleanliness which we are proceeding to corrupt), in the fact that there was, before we laid hands on it, clean air. Our task is to appreciate that grace.

God's creations in the world are his voice, appealing to you and to me not only to join all people of good will in doing what intelligent things we ought to do about the creation, but one thing especially: to love the world and care for it to the glory of God.

The Land

The land is against large-scale changes. Nature is what it is in its ecologically intricate structure because of the long time in which small modifications have occurred and were absorbed into the whole. Recently I was talking with an Iowa farmer about the way intensive land use has changed from what we knew in our youth. Farmers then had a grassy corner of the field where they turned their horses and their plows, and later their tractors, around. My farmer friend recalled that his father taught him to call these unplowed margins "God's frame around the picture."

Now farmers plow right up to the edges of the fence or the ditch. As a result, what we used to call hedgerows—bushes or wild growth around the fields—have been destroyed in large part. This means that the cover for birds is taken away. And birds eat insects; they have them for breakfast, lunch, and dinner.

We have destroyed a situation of natural predation upon insects, and therefore we have to add more things to the land, the plants, and the air to control the insects. Nature is like a fine piece of cloth: you pull a thread here, and it vibrates throughout the whole fabric.

A Working, Joyful Relation

A working, joyful relation to the land has spirited, health-giving power. Around 1684 an old Puritan preacher, William Davenport, said in a famous sermon, "We have been dispatched by God and by history on an errand into the wilderness to create, on this land, a city on a hill, a light in the wilderness to all men." This is a marvelous statement about the promise and hope of the first people who came to this country. They came to this fabulous continent for a fresh opportunity. In some ways the American achievements have been great: we have exercised the American characteristics of goodness of heart, hard work, ingenuity, and cooperative adventurousness. Many good things have come out of the American experience, but we have paid a high price for them in the way we have assaulted the land. Our errand into the wilderness has tempted us to forget the message we were sent to deliver.

Questions for Discussion

1. Share various understandings of the grace of God. How have your understandings changed and developed over time and by experience?

2. Sittler wrote, "God creates his creation in grace. The creation itself is a realm of grace" (p. 3). How does he move us beyond traditional theological definitions of sin and grace?

3. In the section "In the Sixteenth Century" (pp. 8-9), Sittler asks the question: "If grace characterizes the whole of Christian theology, what does this mean for our understanding of the natural world" (p. 9)? What is your response after reading this chapter and again after reading the whole book?

4. Given the advances in medical and bio-technology and the continued assault on the environment, why is it important for Christian theology to develop a theology of nature and grace? What is the connection?

5. Why is the concept of stewardship not strong enough to be a doctrine? How are stewardship's attributes incorporated into a doctrine of nature and grace?

6. How do we make full use of the doctrine of the Holy Trinity and nature in the understanding of who we are?

7. What has kept Lutheran/Protestant theology Christocentric rather than fully Trinitarian? What have we missed or what have we ignored because of the sin/salvation focus?

8. Is Sittler's exploration of nature and grace "up theology" (a human endeavor to reach God) or is it "down theology" (God reaching to humanity)? Explore your responses.

2

Faith: Trust and Risk

The word *faith* is often misused. I remember a form that college students had to fill out. On it was the question, "What faith are you?" They meant Lutheran, Presbyterian, Methodist, or whatever. But Lutheranism is not a faith; it is a particular formation within the family of Christian believers with its own mores, liturgy, confessions. *Faith* must refer to something that is redemptive. A Lutheran church is not redemptive. It may be a servant of the message of redemption, but only God is the redeemer. *Faith* is a word that refers only to an object worthy of absolute trust. It is in God that one must have faith.

We Have No Access

We have no access to Jesus. We have access only to the witnesses of the community that he called into existence by his presence, his person, his power. That is not disputable; that is a fact. I stand in a faith relationship exactly where they stood. They had to believe in him—just as I do. They were no better off than I am, nor I than St. Peter, St. John, St. Thomas. John said, "We have beheld his glory, glory as of the only Son from the Father" (John 1:14). There is no proof of these things. The Christian community arose because its members believed Emmanuel; and they are the ones who reported to us indirectly.

All the theology of the church came later as a way to explicate and account for this reality. The fundamental records are a witness of faith to faith. We stand in the *continuity* of the faith, not of its demonstrable *certainty*. What is demanded of me is no less an act of faith than was demanded of Peter, Paul, or John.

To be a Christian is to sail on perilous seas. We live by faith, and it's never a finished faith. Mine has been collapsed and lying around me in shambles time after time. I've had to stop and reconsider and slowly build it up again, inasmuch as one builds it by oneself.

To build, we reinvestigate, see whether or not the new language can interpret more profoundly the old episodes and words. The task is never done. "I believe; help my unbelief!" (Mark 9:24). That's exactly where we all stand—even Luther, for example. Time and again in his own confessions, Luther talks about moments of what he calls *Anfechtungen*, when he had the horrible fear that he might have been wrong.

We resist the notion that the struggle toward the light is life-long, but that is the fact.

In Recent Years

In recent years, there has been a clamorous demand in theological schools for teaching about spirituality—an interest not characteristic of the Protestant tradition: Spirituality has been dealt with in a formal way mostly in Roman Catholic and Eastern Orthodox courses of study.

What is back of this sudden emergence of interest? One reason it is difficult to comprehend is that there are terms, as there are indeed realities to which the terms point, which are incapable of specification—for which we can have no definition of sufficient inclusiveness that it leaves no remainder. Some things I can define very precisely, but there are words in our language—indeed in every language—that elude definition. The word *imagination* is not capable of definition; yet we all know the word and recognize its referent when it appears. And the word *spirituality*—the power, presence, dynamics of the spirit—is not a definable reality.

We use the word *spirit,* and we recognize the presence that it points to even in the secular use of the word. We talk about such a thing as an American spirit; but it is impossible to define that spirit in terms that are negotiable to someone not an American.

There is certainly such a thing as a French *esprit*. I saw it one day in a humble, but clear, manifestation. During a sabbatical year in Paris I was walking on the street in an old, very poor section of the city, a working people's section. And there came down the street on her way from school a little French girl whose shoes were broken-down and who was dressed in a frock that looked like it had been made from a sewn-up flour sack. She was poor, obviously, but she swung along the avenue with a flower stuck in her black hair and the grace of a princess, as if to say, "Here is a little French girl, and don't you forget it." There is a kind of *élan* in the French spirit that we are all aware of. But when we try to nail the word down, we're in trouble.

In another usage of the word Isaiah said, "The Spirit of the Lord God is upon me" (Isa. 61:1). The Spirit of God is something I cannot define, much less enclose. We so often think of that Spirit as a generally dispersed and gaseous holy presence. It is simply there. We breathe it in, we breathe it out. There is a sense in which the Spirit inheres in all things. There is a sense in which the Spirit of God is simply a wide term for the creative presence of God in everything that God has made.

But note the text, "The Spirit of the Lord God is upon me, because the Lord has anointed me to bring good tidings to the afflicted; . . . to proclaim liberty to the captives." May I suggest with some boldness of interpretation that the Spirit gains specificity in relation to a focal duty, that the Spirit is given with a task. In New Testament times lepers had to be pronounced clean by a priest before they could be readmitted to society. When Jesus told ten lepers crying to him from afar to go show themselves to the priests, he was absurdly promising them that they would no longer be leprous. Yet despite the absurdity of the command and the promise, we read this wonderful sentence: "And as they went, they were cleansed" (Luke 17:14). They did not receive the gift and then take off; they took off in obedience, and the gift was given in relation to the obedience.

The gift of the Spirit is not just a vaporous cloud of unknowing, but the gift is given when obedience is demonstrated. The assignment of a task is the occasion for the specificity of the Spirit; the precision of the gift is accommodated to the acceptance of a duty.

When I was ordained to the ministry, I really didn't feel any particular inbreathing of the Spirit, nor had I ever regarded myself as a very spiritual person (nor do I still so regard myself). But, as my father assured me when I observed that some of my fellow students seemed to have a sure and certain call to the ministry, "There are certain things you can do if you will, and there are certainly those very things that you can do that need doing. How loud do you want it to speak?" In other words, to quote a line from Theodore Roethke's poem, "The Waking": "I wake to sleep, and take my waking slow./I learn by going where I have to go."

When we take on the job, the Spirit is given in relationship to the obedience. The Spirit of the Lord God is upon me because he sent me.

St. Augustine

St. Augustine, at the beginning of his *Confessions*, makes a great and beautiful statement: "Thou has made us for thyself, O Lord, and our hearts are restless until they rest in thee." Back of that statement lies a proposition which says that the human is created for transcendence. It is the Jewish and Christian belief that we are meant for a selfhood that is more than our own selves—that we are by nature created to envision more than we can accomplish, to long for that which is beyond our possibilities.

We are formed for God; we are formed to be in relation to that which was before we were, from which we proceed, and in which we will ultimately end. Faith is a longing. Humankind is created to grasp more than we can grab, to probe for more than we can ever handle or manage.

This transcendental restlessness has two parts. First, I cannot unfold, in the totality of my possibility, to the level of that which I dream. Second, the one who placed the dream in me is the Creator. We are made in the image of God. We are made after the image and the likeness of the ultimate thing itself. Our whole life is an effort to approach, to appreciate, to some degree to participate in, the absoluteness of God himself. But we can never do it; that's why our whole life is a restlessness.

This restlessness may make us want to throw in the towel—or to pull up our socks. You can play it either way. You can either be creatively restless, as before the unknowable, or you can simply collapse into futility. One of the goals of the Christian message is to join together the people of the way, the way of an eternally given restlessness, and to win from that restlessness the participation in God, which is all that our mortality can deliver.

When We Americans Think

When we Americans think of the word *equip*, we conjure up certain images. I am a teacher; I have certain equipment—mainly books—which I must use to do my work. Many years ago I had a little fight with the Internal Revenue Service. I bought the *Oxford English Dictionary*. Every single word in the English language is there, given its meaning with illustrations from English literature starting in Chaucer's time and continuing up to the present. It's a magnificent piece of work, and it cost at that time, secondhand, $300. I deducted it from my income tax under the law that a workman may deduct the cost of his tools (such deductions are now common).

I was called downtown, where a young man behind a desk seemed to have a particularly fussy interpretation of that law: "What's this? You bought a bunch of books costing $300. You can't deduct books under the meaning of that law."

So I said, "Well, why not? If I were a plumber, you would expect me to deduct the cost of wrenches and threaders and elbows. I'm a teacher; words are my business. They're the only tools I have. And if I'm going to do it right, I've got to have the best dictionary I can get."

I'll never forget the astonishment with which he said, "You know, you almost sold me."

"Well," I said, "I want to sell you completely."

He grew tired of my argument, I guess, because he finally said, "Get out of here. It's okay."

We think of equipment as that which we need to do the thing we want or ought or are called to do. However, that is only half the use of the word. If we think of equipment that way, we're thinking of something added on to ourselves. Equipment—*katartismos* in Greek—is also used to mean an internal nurture, an internal formation that matures one's competence for an appointed task. To equip the saints refers in part to certain things that God's followers must add to themselves, as in the great passage, "Stand therefore, having girded your loins with truth, and having put on the breastplate of righteousness" (Eph. 6:14). These are equipment provided by the Lord of the church, by the faith. But the other meaning of the word says to nurture; that is, to cultivate. *Katartizo* is also used in the letter to the Hebrews—inwardly to fulfill: "Now may the God of peace who brought again from the dead our Lord Jesus, the great shepherd of the sheep, by the blood of the eternal covenant, equip you with everything good that you may do his will, working in you that which is pleasing in his sight through Jesus Christ; to whom be glory for ever and ever. Amen" (Heb. 13:20-21).

Just who are these saints? Here again is a word that has become almost stylized by fifteen hundred years of Roman Catholic usage. In the New Testament, "the saints" refers to those who have heard and obeyed, who have had their lives inwardly transformed by what they have heard and believed in the community of faith. Luther has a wonderful sentence about the saints: "To be a saint is to be a forgiven sinner."

In the Roman Catholic hagiography the saints are those who are very special, whose gifts of grace or whose achievements of courage or gallantry, up to the point of martyrdom, have been so esteemed by the church that they have been singled out. But in Luther's sense, saints are forgiven sinners. All Saints' Day is the day when we remember the dead who have preceded us in the great stadium of the church—the "great cloud of witnesses." You and I are saints. In the New Testament sense we are part of the *laos*, the people of God. To equip these sorts of saints does not mean to provide people with exterior additions to their sainthood or to their witness, to their fidelity or their personality, which will somehow be like shoulder pads and helmets. Instead, it means to equip in the internal sense: not an adding-on-to, but a maturation, nurturing, deepening, opening of vision, growing in faith.

In the Internal Processes of Faith

In the internal processes of faith the word *equip* has some relationship to the word *order*. You order your library so you don't have to look through all your books to find the one you want. Or one orders the shop or the bench or the office—whatever kind of place he or she works in. Each person has individual ways of doing this. There are a thousand ways to order things, and only the individual knows what is the right order for him or her; what is order to one person may look like a spattered chaos to another.

I had an aunt who saved boxes. She had to save boxes in order to contain all the other things she saved, and she ordered them with magnificent clarity. The big boxes were all together, regardless of what they held. The little boxes were all together, regardless of what they held. One of the funniest things I ever saw in my life was a little box labeled "pieces of string too short to save." This was order appropriate to the New England mind that never threw anything away.

Order has an interior dimension. One orders one's life according to an intention or a purpose. Fundamentally, we must order ourselves to bring to our lives integrity, which is related to the word *integer,* which means "unity" in Latin. The number one is an integer. It suggests being a harmonious person, an integral person, one who knows where the center is and who works out of that center. This is what it means to have an orderly life of faith, to be equipped as a saint.

Each Person's Pilgrimage

Each person's pilgrimage into a profounder spirituality is a highly personal matter. One's way of probing for depth will be congruent with his or her whole nature. One cannot lay out programs for spirituality. But while spirituality may be personal, it is not individual. There are ways of deepening one's spiritual reflective life that have a universality beyond individual experience.

The concept of order occurs in the Scripture many times. On the first page, we have a cosmos and not a chaos; God created a cosmos by ordering. The biblical literature often marvels at the stars, the moon, and the sun. One of the most common themes in all human reflection is amazement at the fabulous order which characterizes the world: the periodicity of sun and moon and stars, the turning of the seasons.

Human historical life both envisions and longs for an ordering whereby chaos shall be brought into such form as to make an integral personal life, not just a spattering of experience. This longing for order is not just a house-keeping fussiness within the mind; it is a deep thrust within the spirit.

Not only is there a deep human longing for order; there is a command for it. "I am the Lord your God, . . . you shall have no other gods before me" (Deut. 5:6-7). That admonition means that oneness is a focal point which orders the whole chaos. Life is a graduated series of evaluations, doxologies, attestations. I have many interests, concerns, foibles, attitudes. But I must obey that commandment, not only because it is God's commandment but because the structure of life and my own nature demand that I cannot live in disorder. God is the name of the ultimate order. "Seek first the king-dom of God," or to change that into ordinary speech: "Seek first a kingly rule within your life, and all these other things shall be put in their place," said our Lord.

Spirituality

What I am calling spirituality or inwardness cannot be matured by programming. There are helps, there are models, but one cannot teach this kind of thing. One can only speak of occasions when this quality emerges. Look at its indubitable appearance here and here and here, and ask, "By what series of events, by what kind of reflec-tion did this order come to be?" Then translate that into your own life experiences. Here is an example from my experience.

Some years ago I was a member of a group of about twenty who used to meet for discussions. Once we gathered in New Orleans at the home of a Roman Catholic female order. The room for our meeting was down a long hall, and halfway down that hall was the chapel. Every morning as I went down to our meeting, every noon as I went back to my room, early afternoon after lunch when we reassembled, and in the evening, I noticed that the sisters, about thirty of them, were sitting there in that chapel.

There was an absolute silence. They were simply there, four times a day, apparently for a period of fifteen minutes of prayer and meditation. That made me reflect, coming from the much-speaking community of the Lutheran church. I noticed that there in the chapel, there was no leader. In the front of the chapel and over the altar was, of course, a large crucifix. And at that moment I began to wonder, is there any other image in the history of the world that could survive such constant gazing, reflection, and prayer? What other form could absorb all of the worries and apprehensions heaped upon it? Is there any other image in the world that could stand the weight of so profound a demand? And the answer was immediate and obvious: no.

What is it about the figure of the crucified God that has enabled generation after generation, century after century, to sustain so great a weight of human woe? I began to probe and push at the question, and have continued to do so over the years. Why is it possible that from the earliest remains we have of the Christian community, through the great medieval period, into the Reformation, into today's world, the figure of the crucified one upon the cross has been the center of devotional gravity, the center of human pain and torment?

Unless the God before whom we sit, and at whom we gaze, and about whom we think—unless that God has the tormented shape of our human existence, he isn't God enough. We ask, "Why did God become human?" And the answer is that the God who wants to be the source of our order must become the horror of our disorder, or he has no authority.

A marvelous message of the Christian faith is that the eternal order became our disorder and died of it; therefore, he has the right to say, "I am the Lord."

To push a problem in this way until you get some kind of a clarification is one way to grow in depth. Order demands discipline. This need not be a coercive or programmed discipline whereby everybody does the same thing at the same time. But discipline there must be: the discipline of the Roman Catholic sisters; the discipline, before Vatican II at least, of the Roman Catholic priests. You would see them on trains, on buses, with their little zipper-closed, black prayer books or missals, reading every day, as they were obliged to do in the course of the week, all the Psalms. No matter where they were, they'd take out their missal book and read that day's complement. Often it must have been automatic, but the language sinks in. The images percolate. The notions of the language bypass cerebral operations and become part of the organism. The mode whereby order is invited and achieved is not decisive; that discipline and order belong to God is decisive.

We Are Tempted

We are tempted to regard God primarily as a God for solitude and privacy and only secondarily as a God for society. We have a God for my personal ache and hurt, but no God for the problems of human life in the great world. This is where the church has tended to be privatistic, solitary, filled with religious sentiment of a personal kind. We need not abolish that aspect, but it should not have undue importance. We must expand our doctrine of God to acknowledge that he is not only the Lord to whom I flee in times of trouble, but he is also the maker of heaven and earth—God of all that is.

When we say, "I believe in the Holy Spirit, the Lord and giver of life," the reference is not just to religious life, devotional life, prayer-book life. It means all of life.

The Old Shape

The old shape of the confirmation order is now radically inappropriate in its structure; in its culturally formed past it is not adequate to our present circumstances. The culture that formed the order was heavily rural. Most formal education ended with the completion of elementary school. The youth at that school would leave to begin engagements with farms or mills or stores. Hence the age of thirteen or fourteen seemed an appropriate time for a course of religious instruction to wind up. But now in new circumstances, why could we not be theologically inventive and create a fresh rite for that significant moment in the unfolding and maturation of young life? Many people would regard this as being bold beyond what the church ought to do. But the church has always been inventive. Religious faith is not a dull plodding; at its best it is characterized by a soaring inventiveness. However, it seems to me that today we are often too cautious to be creative.

There Are Still Voices

There are still voices abroad today that have the effrontery to suggest that only infallible, inerrant literalism is the Christian way to interpret Scripture. This proposing of a highly peculiar norm for the whole of world Christianity is a strange phenomenon. We ought not to fall for it.

On the first page of the Bible there is an instance of how literalism is but an invitation to transcend the image to which literalism points. That first page is not geology, biology, or paleontology; it is high religion. For there we are told who we are in terms of our constitutive context. And if we could understand that, we would cease worrying about whether the antelopes or the cantaloupes came in a certain order.

The Adoration of God

The adoration of God begins not with Christ, but with the one who made heaven and earth. Jesus never called himself Messiah. He did not claim to be God. He claimed to be of God, from God. But he did not claim to be God.

There are different ways of talking about God. The phrase "son of God" is used in the Old Testament for persons of whom there is no claim of divinity. That is, the term "son of God" is not a biological reference. God is not a biological datum. God does not beget sons as we do. The term "son of God" is a metaphor.

For example, Thomas was a Jew. By virtue of being a Jew he would never call anyone else "God," an unspeakable word to a Jew. When he called Jesus "My Lord and my God," he meant, "That which I understand by the word *God* is certainly here, and this one represents it, or he is the personal presence of it."

But the notion of having an ontological identity, being of one substance, is otherwise. Look at the language of the Nicene Creed. It does not say "one substance," but it says "being of one substance." The word in Greek is *ek*—"God from God, light from light, true God from true

God." The ancient writers carefully avoided making an absolute identity. At the same time they denied a chasm in reality between the two. The reality of God meets us in the reality of Jesus. That's a different statement from saying God and Jesus are an identity.

Even Our Love

Even our love even our generosity, even our self-giving to another, is characterized by a horizontal negation across the positive of love. This becomes terrifyingly clear when we think about our own piety and devotion.

In response to the Lord's command I say my prayers. And when I pray, I am happy that I am doing it. Then I reflect on the happiness I feel, the purity and goodness I feel in being in an act of prayer, and I immediately begin to congratulate myself because I am doing it. And then I think, "That's not right." I then reflect on what a really fine fellow I am after all, because I have the sensitivity to be aware that I ought not so to congratulate myself. I have succeeded only in raising my self-righteousness to a new level.

And then I think next, "That isn't right." But if I know it isn't right, then I also am relieved in part from the guilt, because I know it isn't right.

And the whole interior life goes round and round and round, with deepening ambiguities, which are the burden of being human.

Now this perception of the internal life in its limitations, in its ambiguity, in its egocentricity—this is the human situation. Therefore, God has come to me through that great sign of himself, that condensation of the reality of God, which is the suffering one on the cross. God has to come to me in that way if he's going to be a God who really takes the measure of my heart. If he's going to be what we are in order that we might be reconciled with what he is, he's got to become nothing less than both the promise and the awesome ambiguity of our human life. The interior crossings of myself at prayer are met by God, who comes to me on a cross.

The Affirmation of Faith

The affirmation of faith is not a pure leap into the unknown; one can also have "reasons" for believing, although all reasons are not negotiable or provable. I think the word *certainty* will perhaps have to disappear from the Christian vocabulary—not because our ancestors didn't mean something clear by it, but because the word has by now been permeated with positivism.

I think it's true to say that most of us want what the term pointed to. That is the great appeal of Pentecostalism; its adherents invite you to join the idolatry of provable fact. And if it's really that way, then you don't need faith.

Faith Is a Word

Faith is a word that connects hope and God. As Luther put it, "Faith is trust." And then he added another sentence that is so shocking I rarely hear it quoted. He said "By faith I mean a trust in God's unknown, unfelt, untried goodness and mercy." God is ultimately unknowable. And faith in God is built on precisely his unknowable qualities.

Our Christology

Our Christology is terribly threatened these days by making it into a Jesusology. Jesus is always the presence, the force, the invitatory incarnation of God.

Once at a church where I was interim pastor for a year, there was a woman really hooked on the "me and Jesus" movement, and she used prayer as a kind of personal lubricant to everything she wanted. She worked at a hospital in Chicago, and she used to tell me, "Every morning when I drive from my house to the hospital, I pray to Jesus that he will find me a parking spot. And you know, pastor, he always does." I kept asking myself, "What kind of God-relationship is built on this parking-space-finding Jesus that will sustain this woman in profound deprivation and tragedy? Is it enough?"

One Sunday morning I said to her, "Emma, suppose there is another woman driving in the second lane on the highway taking a sick child to the hospital, and you drive right in to the parking space that Jesus found for you, and this woman who is frantic with a sick child can't find a space. How about her?"

"She didn't pray hard enough," was her retort.

That really stumped me. So I tried to think of how to correct her, but she was immune to argument.

Well, finally I found one, and I am sinfully proud of it; I think it was a straight gift. The next time I saw her I said, "You know this speech you give me about Jesus finding you a parking space, Emma. What do you suppose Mary was praying about jogging along on that donkey on her way to Bethlehem?" Emma never mentioned the topic again. If Mary couldn't find a parking space in which to have a baby, particularly *that* baby, then there must be something wrong with the parking-space-finding Jesus.

Sin

Sin is an unused, unfashionable word, but the facts of life (including my own life) as I look at them—the betrayals, the forgetfulness, the selfishness, the egocentricity—are but the history of humankind written small. There is only one answer to such a vision: it must be accepted. I must simply turn it over to nothing short of grace.

This exposure of the ever-deepening congruity between the mad parables of Jesus, the craziness of the gospel, the incomprehensibility of judgment and grace is the only pattern that seems not to anesthetize, not to cosmetize, the human reality. It seems the only pattern big enough to disclose the raw skeleton of human experience. I cannot prove the truth of the Christian faith, but I cannot escape the haunting congruity between the doctrine of God and grace and love and sin and judgment. The more absurd the human drama becomes, the more appropriate the divine drama discloses itself to be.

Growth in the life of the mind, a lifelong deepening of reflection, may sometimes begin in awkward hesitation—or, equally, in the examination of snappy opinions. If I continue throughout my life to regard with ever-renewed admiration a Rembrandt self-portrait, my mind is not enriched by ever more vehement statements of my admiration. One must, rather, keep pushing the question, "What is admirable about the admirable?" We really do not get to know one another by exchanging catalogs of our likes and dislikes. Real understanding grows with probing.

When one is aware of a hesitation, everything hangs on probing that hesitation. For example, I have never found it possible to include mission to the Jews under the general mission command to the church. As Paul says, "God has not rejected his people whom he foreknew" (Rom. 11:2).

Incessant probing of that moment of hesitation has for me produced a profound deepening in my understanding of Judaism, of the meaning of the law and of the relation of the grace of God given in the law's guidance to God's ancient people, and that grace as actualized and made present in the event of Jesus.

Questions for Discussion

1. List several ways you use the word *faith* in everyday speech. How is faith related to the words *believe* and *religion?* How is faith related to *trust* and *understanding?*

2. Read the section "We Have No Access" (pp. 13-14). What does it mean that "we stand in the *continuity* of the faith, not of its demonstrable *certainty*"? Recall times when your faith "collapsed" and how you "slowly built it up again." How is faith more of a journey than a destination?

3. Read the section "St. Augustine" (pp. 16-17). Do you agree or disagree that humans are "formed to be in relation to that which was [God] before we were"? Explore your answers.

4. At the end of the section "In Recent Years," (pp. 14-16) Sittler says, "When we take on the job, the Spirit is given in relationship to the obedience" (p. 16). How is faith obedience and obedience faith?

5. Read the section "Spirituality" (pp. 21-22). How does contemplation of the "disorder of the cross" become "eternal order" and the subject of our faith and obedience?

6. Read the section "Even Our Love" (p. 25). In what ways is the cross a necessary corrective to an internal life or spirituality? Discuss how Sittler relates and interrelates the doctrines of God, grace, love, sin, and judgment? How do these things have "congruity" (p. 27)? Is Sittler's exploration of faith "up theology" (a human endeavor to reach God) or is it "down theology" (God reaching to humanity)? Explore your responses.

3

The Word of God

Interestingly, no writer of antiquity whom I know anything about ever said, "There is neither male nor female" (Gal. 3:28). Aristotle didn't say it; Socrates didn't say it; Plato didn't say it; Solon, the Greek legal authority, didn't say it. Nobody in the antique world until St. Paul ever expressed such a concept of an absolute erasure of sexual differences.

We Humans

We humans are made for each other. The meaning of the Adam and Eve story, in particular the introduction of the figure of Eve, is not simply to say that it takes two to tango. But the Eve story communicates to all of us the meaning of the German proverb, "Ein Mensch ist kein Mensch." A solitary person is no person; personhood is relation and presupposes another for its actualization. God made a helpmate for Adam. Helpmate doesn't mean a sublieutenant; it simply means that which is necessary for wholeness. On this point, Scripture is very clear—and unique—in its perspective.

Who Is God?

Who is God? Scripture does not answer the question. It's a rather shocking thing to recognize, but Scripture at no point defines God. Rather, it says, "I am the holy one, I am the one who led you through the great and terrible wilderness, delivered you from captivity, called you by your name, made you a people, constituted you an elect nation, a holy priesthood." Or, "I am the one who before the mountains were brought forth, I was. Whatever happened, I did." God in Scripture is not the one who *is* but the one who *does*. This is a functional definition of God, not a dictionary definition.

Scripture never makes any effort to prove God's existence. Further, we do not know who Jesus was from his own statements. Jesus never said, "My relation to God is as follows," or, "My own internal religious feeling is as follows." Jesus never disclosed his interior self; we cannot probe into his psychology. As is true of God, we know who Jesus was only by what he did. We cannot give a definition of Jesus. The only access we have to him is through the reported word about him, and that word is not consistent. A single parable may be given this way in Mark and quite another way in Matthew or Luke. This means that theologically we have to build up the composite of differences, and then try to ask what the church—which knew these differences quite well—meant when it said, "Jesus is Lord."

The Word Became Flesh

The Word became flesh and dwelt among us" (John 1:14). What do we mean when we refer to the Word of God? Primarily we do not mean Scripture; there was a Word of God before there was any Bible. The Hebrew term for word, *davar,* does not primarily mean something we say or write; it means that the creative force of God himself goes out of himself to do something.

There developed a body of literature written by a people who had been made a people by that force, and their writings are called the Word of God. The ultimate meaning of Word is not a document; but the documents were preserved by the ancient Hebrews and the early church because they testified, they bore witness, to the force of the Word. The people had experienced it, and they were transformed by it.

Luther Declared

Luther declared that the mother who teaches the child about the goodness of God, who is the shepherd of all children, is as much a doctor of the Word of God as is the archbishop of Mainz. So when the preacher preaches on "the Word of God," he or she might not quote Scripture. When one declares the presence and the grace of God, the Word is being preached. During the tenth to the twelfth centuries, when virtually no one could read, how did the church continue? The people didn't read Scripture; in fact, many priests didn't either. So they didn't preach Scripture. What they taught was the celebrative worship of God through images and liturgy, hymnody, acts of devotion and tradition. So the church lasted without Scripture.

I've Preached on the Parables

I've preached on the parables for fifty-five years now, and I'm sure that I haven't reached the bottom; in fact, I've begun to doubt that there is a bottom. Every generation reads those parables over and over again in terms of its own questions, and in every case the freshness, the shock of Jesus's teaching, rocks us over and over again. There have been at least ten new books on the parables in the past two or three years; why is that? Not because the parables have to be put into modern English. No matter what kind of English they are in, you can't reduce their puzzling depth.

Take the old Jewish father, reared traditionally, who does what was an incredible thing in a Jewish family: he runs down the road to meet his son who had demanded his part of the boodle and gone off. And now the son comes, full of pot as it were, up the road; and the old Jewish father does a shocking thing that reversed the traditional reverential distance between father and son. He leaves the religious dignity of his role as head of the family and rushes down the road. He seizes the child and calls over his shoulder, "Put on a roast. Get him a ring for his finger and a garment."

Every Jew who read that said, "Come on, that's no way for a Jewish father to behave."

But that's exactly the way Jesus wanted it. He said, "No, that isn't the way it is in life; but I'm talking about the kingdom of God, not about the kingdom of Judea. Cherish your discomfiture."

Do not therefore read the parables as slick little stories of the ordinary; read them rather as they turn the ordinary upside down.

In My Experience

In my experience so many things from biblical speech have entered into the materials of daily life, into reflective possibilities, that I'm not aware they were ever matters of conscious reflection. Time and again phrases come back when you need them, because they were put there before you ever thought you would need them, and they simply got stuck. I once went to a baseball game in New York with Franklin Clark Fry, who loved the New York Yankees next to the Lord, I think. Fry had been brought up, as I had, under a preacher father, and we were both soaked in the Scriptures.

In the ball game, Luis Aparicio, the famous Chicago White Sox shortstop who seldom made an error, did so. "Who can understand his errors?" quipped Fry. Another time, sitting in a meeting of the Ohio synod with Fry before he became president of the United Lutheran Church, a particularly puffy, pontifical character was making a flatulent speech, holding forth much too long, and Fry, quoting the psalm said, "Oh, Lord, we have sinned against thee."

These amusing reflections do not, I trust, divert too much from my point. The ancient vigor, color, sonority of the language of Scripture has a kind of stickiness to the memory. Phrases may remain like forgotten deposits in an account; but they are there for resurrection.

Scripture no longer has an automatic, revered, venerated authority simply because it is Scripture. There was a time when the biblical episodes, stories, and admonitions had an instantaneous and autonomous force because they were in a venerated, traditional book. For almost the whole of Western culture, that time has disappeared. If the authority of the biblical Word is no longer traditionally and generally accepted, or if the authority of the biblical Word is not any longer enthralled in commanding institutions like the church, but is, rather, freewheeling, then the authority we have to appeal to is intrinsically different.

The authority of scriptural words and passages is internal, not external, and it is not automatic. The authority of Scripture has to depend on the text's internal congruity with the human pathos: the reality of what it means to be a human being in this appalling time. The pathos, confusion, ambiguity, and scatteredness of life—this is the situation to which we must address the biblical Word. And that Word will be invested with authority by virtue of its liberating, enlightening, and promising congruity, not by virtue of "the Bible says." For most people, what "the Bible says" is no more authoritative than what *The New York Times* or *The Washington Post* says. The authority must be uncovered as intrinsic.

What Is the Difference?

What is the difference between power and authority? Many exercises of power have no authority. And there are exercises of authority that do their work without power. Richard Nixon had the power of the presidency—up to the moment he resigned. But after the disclosures of his role in Watergate, he had no authority.

On the other hand, Abraham Lincoln never used, except in a few instances, the full power of the presidency; but he had authority. He didn't have to use sheer power. Pius XII, the pope who preceded John XXIII, had and used the full power of the papacy. John XXIII never used the full outer power of the papacy, but he had enormous authority.

What is the difference? Authority is a force continuous with the whole nature and performance of the person or thing possessing it. My grandmother had authority; my grandfather had power. I remember what my grandmother said, and I wanted to do it. I have no remembrance of anything my grandfather said, except that I had to do it.

Scripture has both authority and power. It has great strength, but, most important, we want to do what it commands. That is its authority.

Deal Gently

Deal gently with some things in Scripture, and don't think you have to crack every obscure reference. It has taken three hundred years to write a fairly accurate commentary on Shakespeare's language, and there are some facts that were part of current history in Lancaster or York that are simply gone. We don't know what Shakespeare referred to. Why should we not think that Scripture, written much earlier, contains some passages that are, and probably will remain, unclear?

Questions for Discussion

1. How do we know who God is? What does it mean to "build up a composite of differences" in Scripture to truly know "Jesus is Lord" (p. 31)?

2. Read the section "Luther Declared" (p. 32). What are some ways the Word is proclaimed today without direct quotation of Scripture? Is such proclamation valid? What are some benefits and dangers of such an indirect speech? Share with others your developing understanding of one of the parables of Jesus whose "bottom" (p. 32) you have not yet found.

3. How does Scripture exercise its authority in your life and in the life of your immediate community? Is this authority external or internal? What role does your interpretation of Scripture's authority have in a secular and religiously diverse world?

4. Is the authority of Scripture weaker or stronger if it has to "depend on the text's internal congruity with the human pathos: the reality of what it means to be a human being in this appalling time" (p. 34), rather than an external demand of adherence?

5. Mark an X on the continuum below that best expresses how you rely on Scripture's power and authority. Share your thoughts with others.

POWER   AUTHORITY

6. Explore the difference between and the relationship of power and authority in your life.

7. In what ways do you understand that some passages in Scripture "are, and probably will remain, unclear" (p. 35)? In what ways is that proposition unsettling or reasonable to you? Listen to someone who has an opposite view.

8. Is Sittler's exploration of the Word "up theology" (a human endeavor to reach God) or is it "down theology" (God reaching to humanity)? Explore your responses.

4

Ministry: The Stewardship of the Mystery

The principal work of the ordained ministry is reflection: cultivation of one's penetration into the depth of the Word so that the witness shall be poignant and strong. Clergy have a particular responsibility to the discipline of the reflective life. But they are often negligent in this obligation. It's a terrible temptation to have one's life chopped up by what they tend to call administration, and the temptation must be resisted mightily so as to allow time for the real work of the job.

The Contemporary Church

The contemporary church makes such demands on the minister that the poor individual must sometimes fight for his or her life. Those demands are for a series of virtues and activities that, compressed into one person, constitute an impossibility. One difficulty is in the area of education. If one is going to remain decently familiar with what is needed as a young professional scholar (I don't mean a research scholar), one must be like a good doctor. Most doctors don't do research, but they read the journals that keep them abreast of the research going on.

Most pastors will not do biblical or theological research, nor are they expected to. But most of them don't do what a good doctor does: subscribe to journals, take time to read, engage in programs of study whereby they keep abreast of information necessary to be professionally decent.

Sometimes when I go to a twenty-fifth anniversary of an ordination, or a church anniversary, I spend a few hours with the pastor in his or her study. I often see there the Levitical rule books that the student took away upon seminary graduation twenty-five years ago. But I see no evidence on the coffee table that the literature the pastor attends to is other than the most general reading of the American family. I find this very depressing.

A good teacher teaches her heart out trying to educate people about the excitement of biblical study or archaeology, for example, and then she finds that her students stash it all away and go out and preach sermons that are rich in piety and oversimplification—and the people love it.

At a Conference of Pastors

At a conference of pastors, I sat for two and a half days with a colleague at my side who presented some beautiful, clear, and fresh New Testament studies; he was a complete master of contemporary New Testament scholarship. I was to follow with a theological reflection. We worked very hard.

But while I was at breakfast, lunch, and dinner with these 120-some pastors, never did the conversation turn to what the two of us had been talking about. My colleague was introducing some astounding insights, and I was not exactly unexcited either. But here these pastors sat at meals three times a day and talked about how the walleyes were biting and they were going to have to get a new outboard and their old boat was bad; they would have to put a new roof on their cottage, and the building program at the church was $10,000 behind schedule. Not a blasted word for two and a half days about the topic of that conference.

If I were to attend a professional meeting of gastroenterologists, I'd expect doctors to be there to learn what is going on in that field. At that pastors' conference, the pastors should have been interested in new developments in their professional field.

On the whole I find many pastors dull and soggy in the brain—and I do not apologize for that statement. Ministers are often dull functionaries. Ordination was their intellectual stopping place.

I Was Once Asked to Preach

I was once asked to preach an ordination sermon for a favorite student. As I prepared, I wanted to avoid all past ways of talking about ordination, because many of them I thought were clichés, worn so thin by frequent usage that they slid through the mind like a gelatinous substance on a floor without a rug. I kept looking at the formula for ordination and thinking, "What in keeping the question going is the particular, nonshared, nonsharable, absolutely specific job of this person? Why are we ordaining him to something that is not the same as being a faithful, baptized child of God in Christ's church? What's he got that the rest of us haven't got?"

My questions led me further to ask what actually constitutes the church. It is constituted by two things that do not come out of history, society, human religion, philosophical reflection on ultimate issues, or any human desire or intention. Those two things are Word and sacrament: the gospel as it is transmitted, and the gospel as it is celebrated in the dominical sacraments of the Lord's Supper and Baptism.

The ordained ones—priests, pastors, or ministers—also cannot be other than that which constitutes the church. Therefore I arrived at this conclusion: the ordained ones are the tellers of that story without which the church was not, is not, and cannot continue. They are those who tell the story of those events, promises, and mighty deeds of God that constitute the church.

But cannot others tell the story? The church must keep its story going and assure that there will never be a time or place where the sacraments commanded by Christ are not proffered. Therefore the church insists on preparing a designated cadre to see to it that the constitutive story is told, and that the nurturing sacraments are administered.

This is a way of defining the ordained pastorate of the church that does not elevate it above the laity, but gives it a particular job among the people of God.

The Notion

The notion that everybody has an equal right to authority on all matters is wrong—plain irrational. If I go to graduate school for three years, my judgment on relevant matters should be given a certain weight. My views need not always prevail, but they must be heard. That's my job. I do not have the same right to write a prescription for my dog's bellyache that the animal doctor has, and I can't tell the man who comes in to fix the fireplace how to do it. But I don't think that's any denigration of the people of God.

There are varieties of gifts; and the ordained one is supposed to have been chosen by the church, or at least certified by the church, as having a set of gifts, and he or she must exercise these, while at the same time realizing their limits.

For Reasons of Good Order

For reasons of good order, an ordained minister presides at the Eucharist. But we must not make a theological principle out of a provision for good order. My father, trained in the Joint (Lutheran) Synod of Ohio, began his ministry on the West Coast. He got to the lumber camps only once every three months. A couple of the congregations wanted the sacrament every Sunday, so old Mike Royce administered it. He was a lumberjack. On the frontier we were theologically very direct about some things; and then later we invented all kinds of ways to excuse what would actually be appropriate.

I Come to the Topic

I come to the topic of ministry of the laity out of a genetically sound background. My father, a minister, had dignity; but my mother had the imagination in the family. I remember that she squirmed under the class structure in that old synod: there the laity were clearly the ground troops, and the clergy were the generals.

In the town where I grew up, my mother had great troubles with this. I remember that the district president, a particularly pompous man, came to preach at a conference. It was my turn to babysit (we had a large family) so my mother could go to church. When she returned I asked, "What did he say?"

She replied, "Nothing—for thirty minutes."

I also recall that when my older brother became a physician and began to practice in Chicago, he invited mother to come and visit him. He thought he would shock this woman from a little town in Ohio by taking her to a big city show. So they went to the famous road show, the Ziegfeld Follies. On the stage was a great twelve-foot frame like a book, and as the door opened, the scantily clad ladies came out one by one—to the apparent delight of the audience. My brother thought that my mother would be taken aback by all this. But she was completely unflappable, taking it in stride, and said, "Thank you very much. I enjoyed the show."

Then next spring when the children of the parish school in father's congregation had a program, mother had the local carpenter build a big book, and out of the open book proceeded the little girls, each dressed like one of the women of the Bible. Now with the benefit of this imagination that could go from the Ziegfeld Follies to the Old Testament without batting an eyelash, I had a good early introduction to the ministry of the laity.

What does it mean that not only in the Lutheran church in the United States, but in various other bodies including the Roman Catholic Church, Christians are reinvestigating, reassessing, the meaning of the laity? What is the meaning of the rousing new life that is back of this topic emerging everywhere and with great energy?

First, we must consider the general world liberation movement that includes minority people as well as women. There is something happening in the twentieth century that is, as it were, the broad theater within which the phenomenon we're talking about is but one theological or ecclesiastical aspect.

A sociologist friend of mine was musing about this one night when we were having dinner. He said, "I think the deepest meaning of the 20th century is that the baseline of the human is being enormously broadened." Think of humanity as a pyramidal structure. The baseline at the bottom of the pyramid is reaching upward. People in any culture we know about have always been ordered with very few at the top and then a layer down a few more, and so on. The baseline of billions had very little to do with what was going on at the top.

But what has happened in the twentieth century is that the baseline of the human is swelling economically, politically, demographically, religiously, intellectually. We tend to look at this general liberation as being an indubitable good, and there is a sense in which I think this is true.

But the clear justice of a more general participation in the events and decisions that constitute our lives does not automatically deliver at the top. Twenty million Iranians may be just as wrong as one ayatollah. The American voting population may regard issues with such banality as to end up in the same situation as if one person, a banal leader, made all the decisions. Liberation, as such, does not automatically mean that everyone will be wiser, more prudent, more responsible. It simply means that our stupidity, as well as our prudence, will be distributed among more people.

All of this is relevant to the ministry of the laity; for that theater is not simply an ecclesiastical box or a theological item, though it is that. But it is happening within a general context in which more and more people are joining this ever-striving baseline of human participation in running their own lives.

I think this means that for the foreseeable political future, another one hundred years at least, we're going to have troubled times in the world. You cannot convulsively tear down and then slowly recreate more and more humane forms of human existence. You cannot do that without passing through a time of troubles. But what our late unlamented vice-president, Spiro Agnew, with great unconscious irony, used to call "the decay of our moral fiber" may be the confusion that accompanies all great creative moments in history.

In any case, the theater of our reflections must be broadened beyond simply ecclesiastical concern. My own background in this context is, of course, Lutheran. We Lutherans are not absolutely peculiar human beings, though sometimes some of us act that way. But there is something peculiarly to be perceived and specified about looking at the ministry of the laity from a Lutheran focus.

The Lutheran perspective can contribute to avoiding two pathetic blunders that are characterizing the discussion of the issue in many parts of Christendom. First is that the word *ministry* is an absolutely unqualifiable term. That is, if we say every baptized person is a minister in Christ's church, we are right. But if we become uncritically indiscriminating about that asseveration, we may refuse to recognize forms of ministry within the generalized gift; our demands of ministry will then be unrealistic. There are church bodies in which the word *ministry* is being used in such a way, with such breadth and enthusiasm, that it is almost impossible, without seeming gauche or unspiritual, to introduce any reflective efforts of definition to the various forms of ministry.

Certainly it is imperative to stress the ministry of the laity. As Gustaf Aulen points out in *The Faith of the Christian Church*, from about A.D. 900 to 1200, a legalistic and wooden theory of atonement was being taught in the schools and written in the theological texts. But all the time this thing was being elaborated from the formation of the church, the good people out in front were still singing the vital doctrine of the atonement that is characteristic of the Gospel of Mark: that a strong man enters the prison in which pathetic human life is held by the demons and cracks open the door and brings them out. Aulen notes, "The bishops and the theologians were saying one thing from the front of the church, and the good old laity were singing, 'Christ lag in Todesbanden.'" All of us in our churches rejoice in the fact that the laity are being admitted to all levels of discussion and are invited to all levels of participation in the life of the church. But sometimes we do that on a "professional basis." That is, the lawyers, the business people, the analytical people, the sociologists, the economists, the eggheads among the laity are being brought into the discussion of the church because we need their expertise. Then we rejoice in the liberation of the laity. But we are very selective about which laity we admit—and this is wrong.

Selfhood

Selfhood is not simply finding out and clarifying all the potentialities of the self as individual. There is no selfhood that is not at the same time a self existing in the grid of all selves. I have no self by myself—or for myself. I really have no identity that I can specify except the intersection point of a multitude of things that are not mine. They have been given to me. They are vitalities in history, in human life, and these all intersect at a point which is myself. And yet I know that that self is so richly intersected by others, not only those whom I meet personally but those whom I meet vicariously in the worlds of history and literature, that my self is only a point at which I acknowledge my own presence in the midst of so many things that are transindividual—more than myself.

Such a notion of identity is always in danger of a fateful reduction. I think of the notion of selfhood when I hear my students in their senior year talk about where they would like to exercise their ministry, and I hear them say that what they want most of all is self-fulfillment. There's something rather ghastly about that. I am not ordained to fulfill my precious self. One student had a list of things her first call had to have: it had to be in an urban setting; it had to be with certain kinds of Chicanos, blacks, and poor whites; it had to be in a cultural setting where she could enjoy theater and other activities. I said, "You know, it's as if the Bible says, 'Listen, Lord, thy servant speaketh,' instead of, 'Speak Lord, thy servant heareth.' The church is going to dump you someplace that may have little to do with your agenda. And it will offer the kind of challenge, humiliation, embarrassment, and opportunity that you didn't foresee." Our obedience in ministry cannot be calibrated with an agenda of clamant desires.

I Think

I think how in my own life my preaching has changed in the some fifty-five years I have been at it. Now when I preach, I no longer proclaim: "This is the Word of God and you'd better believe it. The church teaches it; therefore, get with it." In the first place, that tennis ball bounces right back at you. The Word of God has a thundering authority of its own. It must reveal its own reality; it must testify of itself. I cannot hold people to believe on my authority, or the authority of the church. I've got to preach in such a way that the messages of the text—the energies of the reality of God— are disclosed in episode, parable, miracle story, and so on. They've got to do their work by their own intrinsic force, by the truth that they reveal.

Questions for Discussion

1. Briefly list the ministry characteristics of clergy you admire. Circle one or two key attributes that you think are central to the "real work of the job" (p. 37). Share your responses.

2. If Sittler were to visit your study, what evidence would he find that you "keep abreast of information necessary to be professionally decent" (p. 37)? Name two recent biblical studies or theology books or authors that have expanded your professional vision.

3. How does Sittler balance the ordained pastorate and the laity in their mutual ministry to Word and sacrament and the exercise of authority within the church?

4. What successes and failures has "the liberation movement" experienced in the past twenty years? How has Sittler's idea that we cannot tear down and slowly recreate more humane forms of human existence without passing through a time of trouble (p. 43) come true? Relate your response to the post-9/11 world.

5. What peculiar perspectives do Lutherans/Protestants bring to the reflective effort of defining and authenticating the various forms of ministry and the meaning of church?

6. Which does your "Bible" say: "Listen, Lord, thy servant speaketh," or "Speak, Lord, thy servant heareth" (p. 45). Which voice has your ministry heard?

7. How has your proclamation of the gospel changed over the years? What themes do you emphasize more now? On what authority do you now find yourself proclaiming this Word? How is it different than before?

8. Is Sittler's exploration of ministry "up theology" (a human endeavor to reach God) or is it "down theology" (God reaching to humanity)? Explore your responses.

5

Theology: An Accumulation and a Doing

I would suggest that Christian theology is an act of faith whereby we invest a theory of episodes, symbols, metaphors, and historical reality with the most comprehensive meaning and truth we can imagine.

The *truth* of the Christian faith is not severable from the *meaning* of the Christian faith. It is the meaningfulness of a story composed of both the horrors and the delights of human existence. That is fundamentally what the faithful, the church, will depend on for the acceptance of its message. People will be attracted to or repelled by, find interesting or find dull, find relevant or find unintelligible, what we say and teach in exact relationship to its interpretive power.

That is the way Christian theology, in the long haul, has got to understand itself and defend itself. Jesus said that if you will obey and do the deeds, you will know the Spirit of truth (John 14:15-17). That means that the meaning appears only when the risk is taken; one cannot judge it from the outside.

Theology Is Not Just a Church Discipline

Theology is not just a church discipline or a discipline that is exercised by people who are religious. Socrates, Aristotle, Plato, Anaximander were all theologians. Before there were any Christians, there were theologians—people who wondered, to put it in Anaximander's terms, "What is that thing which is before everything, from which everything comes, and to which everything proceeds?"

Christian theology has several branches. First there is "biblical theology," the effort to make a systematic and coherent account of what the Scriptures say about God. It confines itself to the events, history, and statements that are made in the Scriptures, from Genesis to Revelation. Looking at that body of recorded data, human experience, reflection, pathos, and passion, it tries to systematize into understandable concepts what it says about the one who is beyond all others, that ground of all being which is under all that is. Biblical theology is usually subdivided into Old Testament theology and New Testament theology.

Then there are "historical theology"—the effort to record how theology developed from the earliest books of the Bible—and "confessional theology"—which operates primarily within the confessional theological statements of a particular community. Confessional theologians may be interested in theology in general—natural theology, philosophical theology, the theology of the Methodists, the Presbyterians, the Holy Rollers, and so on—but they are primarily concerned with the theology of their own confession.

The kind of theology I do shares with those three other fields. But my coming to maturity as a theologian took place only when I was transferred from the relatively amenable and friendly atmosphere of a church seminary into the slam-bang of a university faculty, where everybody's main response to a statement is, "How come? How do you know it? Why do you say that?" Theology, as I have been called in the last half of my life to practice it, has been carried on as a public activity, having to make its way on the stage of public criticism and public knowledge, amidst disciplines like physics, chemistry, mathematics, sociology, anthropology, and linguistics—and that is a difficult place to be a theologian.

My job at the University of Chicago was called *constructive theology*. My responsibility required that I, as both an individual and a representative of the community of faith, put that tradition on the battle line where theological affirmations meet general human affirmations: to reason and construct forward into a new situation the old statements of the church and the believing community.

For instance, I can say for myself and within my own community, "I believe in God, the Father almighty, creator of heaven and earth. I believe in Jesus Christ, his only Son, our Lord," and people nod their heads in a corporeal and corporate affirmation. They too affirm that. But in the university, the moment I say, "I believe in God," somebody says, "Why? By what right? By what reasonable ground do you dare say a thing like that?" So I have to take the whole tradition of accumulated Christian thought and put it forward as a public event in the face of those who don't believe it or who don't know whether they believe it. Theologians or preachers cannot make people believe. They can only explicate what it might mean to believe, in such a way as to lead others to entertain the possibility of believing.

I can offer an illustration. I was teaching in a typical class made up of all sorts of men and women, some of them believers and some nonbelievers. (Not everyone who comes to a theological school in a university is headed for ordination; most of them are going to be teachers.) I was lecturing on the magnificent statement in the Nicene Creed about the relationship of Jesus the Son to the Father. A student sat there watching me with gimlet eyes. When I came near the conclusion, he raised his hand.

I said, "Okay, what is it?"

He said, "You know, if it were true, it would do."

Now that is as far as a teacher can go. I can't transmit my sense of the truth of that statement to him, like writing out a prescription and letting him follow it. I can only teach in such a way as to engender in him the questions, as if he were saying to himself, "If it were true, it's a big enough truth that it would pull me together." In a sense, that's what a sermon is for: to hang the holy possible in front of the mind of the listeners and lead them to that wonderful moment when they say, "If it were true, it would do." To pass from that to belief is the work of the Holy Spirit, not of the preacher or the teacher.

A constructive theologian has a second job. He or she is supposed not simply to teach, transmit, and elaborate, but also to ask what meaning such a statement would have in view of the contemporary situation. That is to say, theology is not an accumulation only; it is a work. It is not just what people have thought, but it also investigates how the church's message might make sense, how its truth might be made clear, given the body of new learning in our generation.

For example, think of what enormous changes have taken place in the past thirty years in the study of cosmology. We now know, as we did not know so clearly when I was a boy, something about the enormous distances of the universe. We know a great deal that we did not know in the beginning of the twentieth century about the various forms and activities of energy. We know a lot about the history of the cosmos. All of this must be admitted to the theater of theological reflection.

At the School

At the school with which I am now connected, they call me O. B.— Old Brooder. My main task is to sit and think. I am aided in that effort by the fact that my vision is now so bad that I cannot read. And while I lament that fact, I am also happy in certain fringe benefits (in fact, they're not fringe, they're central). When one cannot enjoy the constant input that reading affords, but must, as I do now, depend on readers and tapes, one has to think more about less. And I've found that in recent years I have probed more deeply into and reformulated for myself much in the church's theological tradition.

By *theology* I mean a reflection over and over and over again on the elemental events of the Christian community: the entire history of Israel that stands back of the events informing the new Israel. Those events, as they have been recalled and celebrated repeatedly throughout history, are like a certain amount of money put in a savings account. They accumulate an increment through the centuries. This accumulation is not like that of a tapeworm, sending out segment after segment of its own energy. The accumulation of theological terms, ideas, images happens because the remembered events are always encountering new situations in the human family, in the social world through history. They are not only pushed toward ever greater richness; they are drawn by events into ever fresh reflection.

When we talk of *theology*, we mean not only an accumulated mass of devotion, piety, reflection, intellectual work, historical documents. By *theology* we mean not only a having but a doing—not only an accumulated tradition, but a present task which must be done on the playing field of each generation in actual life. One *has* a theology, to a greater or lesser extent, in order to *do* theology, in order to exercise, administer, manifest this always forward movement.

I want to do theology in such a fashion that the mind may be invited to ask what is the relationship between the church and what I affirm about God and Christ. How does that illuminate some circumstance in culture? I do theology that way not simply because I chose to—although had I been utterly free of circumstances, I think I would have chosen it that way—but I do it quite frankly by accident. All my teaching career and my thirteen years in the pastorate were lived on the margin of the church's life, where the church meets the world. My pastorate, during the very heart of the Depression, was in a little, beat-up, segmented congregation. I was ordained the week the stock market crashed; 70 percent of my people eventually were out of work in the midst of a great industrial city.

In my church we had no nursery, no crying room, no couple's club; we didn't have anything but a room, a hymnal, a pulpit, and an altar. So my early experience was never insulated or encapsulated within the church. I had to do theology on the street, where intellectual and cultural events were always pouring in on me.

The Church

The church is no longer standing astride Western culture celebrating theology, the queen of the sciences, in command of a powerful, commonly believed tradition. Most people today not only do not believe the Christian faith; they do not know what its claims are.

We live in what has been called a Kleenex culture: build it, use it, throw it away. The very changes in our architecture are parabolic of the changes in the culture. Our technological society has determined that buildings are no longer solidifications of a tradition; they are simply functional housing for an operation. That's true not only of church buildings but of everything else. The Sears Tower in Chicago is estimated to be built for about half a century. And then the thing will be knocked down, and they'll build something equally bad.

The fundamental affirmations of Christian theology do not, like the Sears Tower, have a fifty-year life span. But the language of their transmission, the images and human realities that constitute their proclaimed substance, must find their vocabulary and manner always in relation to the changing world.

Theology for the Laity

The term "theology for the laity" is a phrase that invites the mind to a wrong image. The phrase suggests that really important theology is done in relative seclusion by special persons who command appropriate skills and write theological texts. This material, so the image suggests, is rare, difficult, often abstract, and unavailable to the ordinary believer. So we further erroneously suppose that this good stuff must be watered down, reduced to obvious banalities, and retailed on Sunday morning to the patient customers.

Such a notion is both untrue and unfair. The academic theologian, like a researcher in any recondite body of knowledge, has the lonely obligation to use special skills to recover, clarify, order, and fashion appropriate conceptions.

A "theology for the laity" does not dilute that substance, banalize or oversimplify those findings, or make an obvious cliché out of a profound parable or other statement of Jesus. Theology for the laity is an exercise in language and reference whereby real substance intersects ordinary experience. "The fodder must be put down where the sheep can nibble," said Luther. But it must be real fodder.

My Theology
My theology is not one derived from nature, it is a theology of the incarnation applied to nature which is quite different.

I Think
I think it is because I came into theological work via the parish that I have always tested the usefulness of my own theological statements by their transmissability in the sermon—whether I could make sense of this thing to the faces that sat there on Sunday morning looking up at me.

My Theological Career
My theological career has been a not-wholly-successful effort to drag my students out of the church—out of the church!—into what is happening in the world. My general effort was to lead them to appreciate the reality of the natural, the historical, the cosmological world of the galaxies in order that their theological speech would be intersective of the world their listeners take for granted.

Christian Theology
Christian theology says that a person's being, selfhood, sense of who he or she is, is constituted by relationships in such a way that if any one of them is damaged, the individual's being is damaged.

Think about the word *being*. We're all used to the word *existence*. I can talk about my own existence, and I can point to the particularity of my autobiographical record. There is such a thing as the particularity of my existence over against yours; each of us can say this of himself or herself: "I was born in a particular place; I grew up with specific parents, went to certain schools."

But when I talk to you of *being*, I can only talk to you out of my existence and fling words across to the strangeness of your existence, which is in many ways other than mine. But I can do that and be understood because we have something in common that transcends the particularity of our existence.

What do we have that makes it possible to talk to one another? This is what we mean by being, human being, the essence or core of likeness that permits language and intelligibility, even if we have no language in common. For example, if I'm walking down a street in Bangalore, and a fat and pompous character struts out of a bank and slips on a banana peel, the observing Indian will laugh as loudly as I do. This response arises out of the depths of our being. All of life traverses a banana peel, and we all know it, whether in India, East Asia, Iceland, or Chicago. Christian theology affirms our connectedness.

Questions for Discussion

1. How does Sittler's exploration of Christian theology as imaginative interpretation in search of truth and meaning (p. 48) influence people inside and outside of the church?

2. Do you have faith? Why? How do you know it? How can you say your faith is true? On what authority do you make your claim? Is your faith a big enough truth? Reflect on your own theological suppositions and foundations.

3. In the section "At the School" (pp. 51-52), Sittler wrote: "One *has* a theology, to a greater or lesser extent, in order to *do* theology" (p. 52). What does it mean to do theology as opposed to have a theology?

4. What is Sittler's notion of "theology for the laity"? By what can one test its usefulness and effectiveness? Evaluate your own notion and practice of "theology for the laity."

5. Reflecting on the last four sections of this chapter (pp. 54-55), what do we have that makes it possible to talk to one another? Is it what we mean by "being"? How is "being" theology?

6. Sittler wrote, "My theology is not one derived from nature; it is a theology of the incarnation applied to nature" (p. 54). How does that distinction make a difference?

7. Is Sittler's exploration of doing theology "up theology" (a human endeavor to reach God) or is it "down theology" (God reaching to humanity)? Explore your responses.

6

Moral Discourse in a Nuclear Age

In each succeeding generation ethical issues demand ever deeper insight. Our parents knew as well as we that the Christian obligation is to hear the will of God and do it. In most instances, they could find laws, biblical precedents, comparable instances and analogies whereby to guide their steps. They could ask with a certain admirable directness, "What does the Word of God teach concerning these matters?" We must ask the same question, but we cannot with equal clarity discern a guiding counsel for many problems of our time. Neither Scripture nor the body of Christian tradition can be transposed with adequate clarity into the tangled web of contemporary life. Fresh approaches are needed.

A dramatic instance of this need is the issue of death and dying. Contemporary medical knowledge makes possible the deferral of death by various means. The circumstances created within a family by the critical illness of a member are both clear and pathetic. The other members wish to obey the will of God, and they look to both Scripture and church tradition to furnish them with guidance, but neither Scripture nor tradition knows about the techniques of contemporary biological science and medical technology. Neither unambiguously tells us what we ought to do about genetically damaged fetuses, or what decision to make about continuing treatment for terminally ill grandparents. Faced with such situations, we are required to make absolute decisions between absolute options ("to live or let die"), and these absolutes must be obeyed within absolute indeterminacy.

The Unenvisioned Possible

The parables of Jesus have been critically established as being the closest we can possibly come to the eventful reality of Jesus himself—what he intended, what he purposed, what he determined to say and to be. Most of the parables begin, "Now the kingdom of God is like . . ." or "The kingdom of God is as if. . . ." This opening is followed by a narrative. These narratives—often understood as illustrations, exemplary stories, or moral lessons—have through the centuries exuded inexhaustible invitations to reflection and even bewilderment. Their boundless vitality is the secret of their allure and the threat of their judgment. They are not, as we might wish, "perfectly clear." They invite trouble, they judge, and they promise; and they do all this with a continuing energy and pointedness that grasp us in every situation.

The parables of the kingdom are a kind of surgical exploration of those modes and postures of sin that blind, corrupt, and pervert humanity's relationship to God. Unless our Christian moral discourse permits the power of the parables to question and then correct that central perversion, we will continue to regard them merely as interesting illustrations and, in the process, pull the teeth of their intention. For they all say that the absolute permeation of our human condition by the power of sin, which all of us are loath to acknowledge, is the only acknowledgment whereby our redemption can be envisioned and received. The parables shock the mind into opening to the unenvisioned possible; they madly exaggerate in order to jolt the consciousness of the religiously secure; they are an assault upon the obvious. The entire momentum of conventional piety is brought into question: the man sells everything for the one thing; the shepherd leaves the ninety-nine undefended in order to find the lost one; in defiance of common sense, the woman takes the house apart to find the lost coin; the lord commends the unjust steward for his uncanny perception of the truth. Is it not possible that the accounts of the miracles are enacted forms of the parables? The parables are spoken miracles; the miracles are enacted parables.

Inasmuch as the people of God strive to discern God's will in every situation and to pray for the gifts of grace to receive it, and inasmuch as Jesus most succinctly speaks of this will of God in the parables, may it not follow that a Christian mode of ethical discourse might be most fruitfully suggested by a never-ending attention to these parables? This way of inquiry is particularly apposite as the church probes for a proper response to the immensely complex issues of peacemaking and peacekeeping. For here the question of right obedience mirrors on a huge scale precisely the tormenting problems we confront on a small scale when we ask the bedside question, "To live or let die?"

Speech in a Nuclear Age

To illustrate more concretely what may be suggested by the term "fresh modes of moral reflection," we may bring under scrutiny several terms central to the politics of living in a nuclear age, terms that occur in every sober discussion of peacekeeping.

It is alleged that deterrence, guaranteed threats of unacceptable harm between conflicting nation-states, averts actual warfare between the superpowers, diverting attention to other means of resolving conflicts. Deterrence is seen as holding in check the violent impulses on both sides. This term has achieved a strange reputation for cool rationality. Our confidence in the idea and the policy of deterrence is soberly maintained against all the evidence to the contrary. For in fact, deterrence does not deter. The madness of trying to avert death by the multiplication of its means only evokes ongoing escalations of the arms race. Power, believed to be a deterrent, always invites the development of a more threatening counterpower. The invention of the stirrup gave mounted warriors greater strength; the fabrication of armor was the rejoinder. Big guns could sink wooden ships; iron plates were the rejoinder. The machine gun multiplied fire power; tanks were invented. Aircraft begot antiair-craft. Big bombs became the superbombs dropped on Hiroshima. Moral generalities are hazardous, but this one is clear: angry and prideful people will envision, devise, and use whatever will destroy the enemy. There is no ground for confidence that current specula-tions about extending our earthly obscenities to the heavens would accomplish anything but an equivalent rejoinder, and thus infect with our evil the unoffending stars.

The uncritical acceptance of the self-deception implied in the term *deterrence* and the clear history of the failure of such a policy suggest that the terms *irrational* and *unrealistic*, which are often used with Olympian confidence to dismiss all who would suggest radically new possibilities for human communities, have lost all *rational* mean-ing. In fact, a strange and parabolic reversal has occurred in our time. Until recently, notes Paul G. Johnson in a *The Christian Century* arti-cle ("The Bifocaled Lutheran Vision of Peace," December 21-28, 1983, p. 1178), it has been the "dreamers" and "idealists" who opposed war and held out visions for a peaceful world, and the "real-ists" who accepted war as tragically inevitable for the human species. Now, writes Johnson, the tables have been turned. It has become the starkest "realism" to acknowledge that the world will be blown up if we do nothing to stop nuclear madness, and the thinnest "dream" to suppose that anything short of nuclear disarmament can avert this catastrophe. If two angry persons were to confront each other with weapons of mutually assured destruction, and if one of them were a so-called utopian dreamer who mused that "there must be some other way . . . ," the term *rational* might more becomingly be used of the dreamer than of the opposing *realist*.

The possibility here for a fresh mode of moral reflection is exactly like that which haunts us in the parables of Jesus. In those stories the new, the possible, the mad reversal of our expectations constitute the enduring promise and mind-tormenting power of the biblical Word. Such theological pondering of the Word is methodologically more appropriate than the proof-text snippets marshaled as evidence to nail down conventional moralities. In the words of W. H. Auden's "Christmas Oratorio," *For the Time Being*, "Nothing can save us that is possible. We who are about to die demand a miracle."

Deterrence also implies that the other side is evil and cannot be trusted, whereas our side is good. To postulate a dichotomy that sees the evil as primarily the character of the *other* is the sly and fateful way our self-deception operates. Evil is never more quietly powerful than in the assumption that it resides elsewhere. The term "evil empire" is a description of all empires. The internal empire of every person's egocentricity is the template of historical evil.

The word *verification* is currently used to say that if I make a contract with my neighbor to follow agreed-upon procedures, that contract must be secured by our mutual ability empirically to check compliance. In such a contract the term is clear and the necessity obvious. When, however, the term is transferred to the realm of moral discourse, the adjective *moral* both indicates and describes a radically new context. That context both presupposes and requires that the element of trust decisively modify the spirit as well as the expectations of the conferring persons.

What I cannot trust I must verify. But if I must verify in order to converse, I have not a conversation but a purely calculated negotiation in which every possibility for movement is annihilated by the minutiae of tit-for-tat. All genuine trust implies risk. All human relations go beyond the verifiable, and unspokenly assume that the hopes, the needs, the longings of the other are not utterly discontinuous with one's own. Indeed, my own self-interest demands and is commonly characterized by such an assumption. I do not verify my physician's statement that the treatment he prescribes is based on his scientific reading of the data, or question that his professional self-interest is on the side of telling the truth. In an even more fundamental relationship, a man and a woman do not verify their conjugal promises, nor insist on verification in every aspect of their relationship. They trust one another. It is not here suggested that trust can replace the conventions of treaty obligations in pacts between nations, but it is suggested that even within such transindividual relationships, the assumption of the continuities of elemental human desires, fears, and visions of a better world does exist and operate. At the very least the rigidity of our stereotypes of other nations must be modified by the sheer dynamism of historical change. Should we continue to deal with the U.S.S.R. as if Stalin were still the boss?

The Obligation to Justice

In the very considerable literature on peace and politics, the term *peace* is commonly used as if it referred to a disengaged and highly desirable virtue, achievement, or gift hanging in splendid and beguiling isolation. Such an assumption oversimplifies. It suggests the notion of an exclusively interior and private serenity, a well-insulated tranquility achieved by detachment. By *peace* the devout often mean the bovine contentment sustained only by a virtual ignorance or dismissal of all that maddens, saddens, and gladdens the generality of human-kind.

Among Christians, *peace* dare not be used in this antiseptic way. The peace of God is more profound. In the Scriptures, peace has meanings so many and various that they cannot be condensed into a single statement; all such meanings operate within a context, and that context always involves discipline, choices, denials, sacrifices.

These choices can be illustrated by scrutinizing our motives and those of our fellows as we inquire why we want peace. When, not long ago, I saw a group of women from a wealthy suburb of my city marching in a peace rally and observed the elegance of their expensive attire, their Gucci shoes, and the waiting chauffeur-driven cars at the edge of the square, I could not but recall the statement of a wise man: "Everybody wants peace. But we also want what we cannot have without war." We all want to sustain the standard of living we have become accustomed to. We all want our proud nation to be number one. We all want to maintain access to minerals and fuels, no matter where located, that are the necessary components of our technologically advanced society. In other words, though we all want peace, we also want one system or another that allows the fulfillment of our wishes, wants, and delights to continue unabated. We want our peace. But the peace that God wills cannot be given when we understand peace only in egocentric terms. The power of the strong to control what they want evokes an outcry from the weak.

Throughout the Scriptures, love, righteousness, and justice are a trinity of terms that swirl around and penetrate each other. In one passage or another, each may have a primary reference, but its context almost always pushes out to enlarge its meaning through reference to the others. The righteousness of God is not separable from his will to reconcile all creation to himself, and that reconciliation presupposes love and justice. The works of love are never specified apart from the obligation to regard and deal with the other with justice.

The coexistence and interplay of these terms is illuminating when, as in our present inquiry into "peace and politics," we properly place strong emphasis on the power of love. What is the nature of this love that throughout the Scriptures is affirmed to be fundamental to the nature of God himself? A barrier to a comprehensive understanding of love is our attempt to grasp the fullness of its meaning by comparing it to mutual love in intimate personal relations. We grope for an adequate understanding from the perspective of our own purely individual and private experience of love.

But love is not merely an affection. Love's surplusage is disclosed when we puzzle over Jesus's statement, "A new commandment I give to you, that you love one another" (John 13:34). That love is commanded is puzzling. As we clearly know, love cannot be commanded. It emerges, occurs—we "fall in love." There is something incomprehensible in all instances of our human love. But Jesus nevertheless commands it. What kind of love is this?

I am not told that I am to *like* my neighbor; I am ordered to *love* him or her. Luther's explication of our relation to the neighbor brings us close to a right understanding. Our neighbors, in the biblical sense, are those persons who live in God's creation with us in the solidarity of our life together on this earth. Though I cannot will myself to feel an oceanic affection for all people, I can acknowledge my bond with the whole of creation. In that bond I am to recognize the authenticity, the *thereness*, the concrete life and existence of the other.

In the broad context of human solidarity the exercise of love is realized in transaffectional justice. Real love grasps the hand that need holds out. Needs cry out from millions I will never meet. Justice is love operating at a distance. When, for instance, my church tells me that millions of people are starving and that it is my duty to show my love for them through helpful actions, I become aware of the transindividual meaning of love. I cannot feel any immediate affection for two million people. Love becomes a recognition of the neighbor in his or her need, and takes the transpersonal form of distributed food.

Just as love is transposed into acknowledgment, and hence can be commanded, so the term *justice* can be opened up when pondered in continuity with this commanded love. Even in pre-Christian and non-Christian discourse, the term *justice* affirms people's solidarity within a shared theater of existence that absolutely requires order, limit, and the acknowledgment of rights. Justice is not an invented and imposed virtue; it is a precondition for human life. The Old Testament does not create the idea or the term. It presupposes that ordering and ascribes it to God the Creator. That order is an aspect of God's righteousness; its denial brings one under God's judgment. The prophets' vehemence and the cutting clarity of their judgment makes clear that injustice is blasphemy before the holy, not just failure before the civil.

Consequently, it is clear that any envisionment of peace that is purely interior and dispositional—as a kind of tranquil ambience for the inner life—is a disastrous reduction. It is equally clear that peace is impossible without transforming the meaning and exercise of love beyond its egocentric theater, and that any exercise of love that does not intersect and demand the primal human dignity and world-ordering called *justice* is futile.

A Proposal

It is exactly the parables' cogency in giving us a vision of what a "fresh mode of moral discourse" might provide that suggests the following proposal. The genius of the parables is their insistence on the power of God's possible. The envisionment of the possible haunts the mind into the quest for fresh ways of dealing with the indeterminate character of our moral quandaries.

At present most churches have no continuing structure to deal with the kind of issues described here. As issues arise and the demand for guidance becomes clamant, we assemble an ad hoc study. A different issue convokes another conference. Would it not be possible for each communion to establish an ongoing "Commission on Theology and Ethics"? Such a commission could deepen and refine the continuing reflection of a community of conversation. It should include not only the church's scholars, but also those nonacademic persons whose intelligence, concern, sensibility, specialized knowledge, and spiritual endowments might serve to invite scholarship into the more ample and immediate phenomena and language of the common life. An additional virtue of such a commission would be its possibility for perceiving and specifying such fresh modes of moral discourse as the circumstances require.

Twentieth-century modes of thought, life, and work present us with new issues for moral reflection. Problems arising from advances in the biological sciences are but one example of such emerging and pressing moral issues. A continuing communal process of moral discourse would create a fermenting compost heap of reflection within which the modes of thought sharpened by dealing with one issue could penetrate and illuminate another.

Questions for Discussion

1. Sittler wrote this chapter as an article for *The Christian Century* (March 6, 1985) in the waning years of the Cold War. What do you think are the major moral issues facing us in the growing threats of a post-9/11 world?

2. What does Sittler mean that "we are required to make absolute decisions between absolute options, and these absolutes must be obeyed within absolute indeterminacy" (p. 57)?

3. What function do Jesus's parables perform in moral discourse? How is this function different from a more traditional understanding?

4. Sittler explores political words from the Cold War era. How are these words used today in our political/diplomatic speech? What new words are accepted uncritically in today's moral discourse and political statements, as were the Cold War words?

5. Compare and contrast the way "peace" is used in political/secular speech and the way Sittler wants Christians to use the word. Who is at the center of "political peace," and who is at the center of "theological peace"?

6. How does Sittler's proposal (p. 65) for Commissions on Theology and Ethics fit in a post-9/11 world when the threat is indeterminate terrorism by various groups and not nation-against-nation military conflict? How should the church engage in moral discourse in determining a response to non-nation state entities?

7. How have extremist insurgencies, such as al-Qaida, brought about a new "nuclear age" that requires a new form of moral discourse? Is the threat from these groups more or less frightening than that posed by the superpowers' nuclear weapons? Explore your responses.

8. What hope does Sittler offer those who seek peace and justice in today's world?

7

Aging: A Summing Up
and a Letting Go

Aging has been called "an awkward problem." The dramatic growth in sheer numbers and in longevity of the world population has excited students from many disciplines—demographers, anthropologists, sociologists, psychologists, educators, politicians, philosophers, theologians, and all the specialists within the general category of medicine. An article in *The New England Journal of Medicine* ("Benefit and Cost Analysis in Geriatric Care" by Jerry Avorn, M.D., May 17, 1984) describes and critically analyzes the three major proposals for dealing with the problem of how most justly to relate health resources to fresh circumstances. An interesting paragraph near the end of that essay provides me with an appropriate entrance into the issue I want to discuss here. "Little comfort can be found in the standard argument that decisions on resource allocation are made on the basis of 'gut feelings' all the time, and that these methods are an improvement over such imprecision. Approximate as gut feelings may be, they remain superior to delusional systems, no matter how detailed they are."

The capacious phrase "gut feelings" seeks to scoop up all the phenomena of aging that slip through the technological grid of the method that informs all the proposals so carefully described. That method is empirical, demographic-statistical, rich in elaboration of physical data. It is a method that, since Descartes, has achieved an almost absolute dominance as a way to study and envision programs for the solutions of all human problems. The arrogance with which this method is calmly applied is, of course, sustained with slight embarrassment by its massive success since the days of the Enlightenment. The submersion of qualitative realities into the heady solution of quantitative methods has in our time reached the state for which Hannah Arendt's term *banality* is alone adequate. It is inevitable that the exercise of this method in the determination of models for health care for the aging should elevate the term *productivity* to normative status. Productivity thus conceived is really equivalent to worth. Indeed, this essay boldly identifies personal worth with the kind of productivity that can be specified in dollar value. This strange calculus is not only offensive to moral sensibility; it represents so radical a compression of a large term as also to offend common sense. John Keats, in utter poverty and fatally ill the last two years of his short life, composed in those few months the odes which secure his place among the great poets.

So we return to the question. Why is aging an *awkward* problem? The term is commonly used to designate aspects of a situation for which conventional modes are felt wanting, circumstances for which usual procedures are inappropriate. We sometimes use the word *awkward* to describe a social or interpersonal situation in which the unexpected upsets the anticipated. The fact that human life has a limit, that life moves inexorably toward death, is to the common mind of a technically informed culture of the West an awkward fact, for our entire educational system is geared to the transmission of problem-solving techniques and devices. Popular culture is invited to assume that knowledge, resolution, time, and an adequate allocation of funds can solve all problems. A branch of the American armed forces in the Second World War invented an interesting maxim: "The difficult we do at once; the impossible takes a little longer." Professor Hans Jonas once wrote an essay in which he mused over the disposition of our generation to regard death as an awkward interruption of a play that was so pleasantly getting on very well. Human life has been increasingly brought under such managerial powers as to make death a cheat, a ludicrous interruption, an event for which an entire profession has conspired to cosmetize the dead and narcotize the survivors.

No brief essay can designate or adequately describe those interior dimensions of aging to which I have alluded as determining the awkwardness that inheres in the methodological models. But some of these may be pointed to and given a voice. On the assumption that the memorable literature of the human family is the most enduring confessional of human inwardness, I have for several years been collecting such expressions. I am astonished at the plenitude, the force, the variety, and the eloquence of these sentences. From Homer to the literature of our present moment, the huge mass is richly strewn with the reality of aging giving voice to a ductile, but awesome and universal, interior truth that is not capable of quantification. The most deeply human is not amenable to digital reduction.

Several themes are central, pervasive, and many-voiced. The fundamental feeling that colors the affective life of all of us who are at or beyond the biblical "three score and ten" can best be designated by the term *pathos*. Pathos is not a simple thing; it is an ever-more acute sense of passingness, of the urgency of unretrievable time, the knowledge that time leans forward, a sense that the recurring events of life have a limit—this place I may not see again, this one I may never greet again, this little company around the table may never again around another table meet. The interior sensibility of aging is made pathetic by a radical elimination of all those relationships and components that have constituted one's life world. John Donne's "Every man's death diminishes me" leaps from formal fact to individual experience with terrifying force. The network of personal relationships constitutes the interior tonality of a life, and the fragility of these relationships is recognized in old age with particular hurt. The quiet departures within this personal world are snapped like filaments in the web of identity.

I know no statement of the pathos of the aging spirit more rich and true than the opening lines of William Shakespeare's Sonnet 73. The common image out of which these lines distill their beauty and velocity is the image of a springtime green tree alive with the voices of birds, and that same tree against a sullen, autumnal sky when October shall have come again.

That time of year thou mayst in me behold
When yellow leaves, or none, or few, do hang
Upon those boughs which shake against the cold,
Bare ruin'd choirs where late the sweet birds sang.

These lines are not the statement of a problem awaiting solution; they are, rather, a statement of the human condition for which there is no solution. The demand is, rather, for courage, acquiescence, resignation, acceptance—some coming to terms with. They are a time of remembering, gathering up and sorting out, discriminating between the abiding and the evanescent, a time of perhaps unmarked passage from knowledge to wisdom, from simple awareness to insight, to what Jonathan Edwards called "consent to being," to the psalmist's "so teach us to number our days that we may get a heart of wisdom," a movement of the total spirit from an anxious hanging on to a graceful letting be, a releasement.

If this were an essay of another sort I could elaborate my own transaction within this awkwardness. But the purpose of this short piece is rather a transpersonal one: to state a problem in terms appropriate to its universality and its profundity, and thus to suggest that discussions of health and medicine achieve a wise sense of humor whereby to modify their often brusque proposals.

My First Parish

When I was in my first parish in Cleveland, I spent some time with Walter Holtkamp, Melville Smith, and others at the Holtkamp Shop, which was creating the first American Baroque organ. I learned something about organ building and voicing, and I helped install the first Baroque pipe organ in America in the Cleveland Museum of Art. I turned the pages for Albert Schweitzer when he inaugurated it with the Franck "Chorale in A Minor."

I spoke with Walter Holtkamp Jr. recently about those early days when organ builders sought above everything to get clarity in the organ tone so that there wasn't a big sonorous romantic mush but clear voices to articulate the polyphonic music of the period of Bach and Buxtehude. "Well," he said, "I've got news for you! They don't even want clarity anymore. The new generation *wants* mush. The more romantic and mushy you can make it, the better they like it."

This evoked a deep sadness in me, but I won't try to understand it. The older I get, the fewer things I understand. Some of you may have heard of the response from a famous literary figure who, upon the acceptance of a prestigious award near the end of his life, was asked to make a brief statement. He said: "I'm an old man; it's a strange world; I don't understand a damn thing." The older I get, the more sympathy I have with this sentiment.

Old Age

Old age is a time of gathering diminishments. The maturation of hope and expectation into experience reverses in aging. There is literally no future. All the little filaments of personal relations that constitute your world snap loose, one after another.

I think of the world in which I was an active teacher and churchman and worker. Ted Tappert, Franklin Fry, Paul Krauss, Willem Visser 't Hooft—all that company of world theologians of which I was not a peer, but a little guy among the greats—Reinhold and Richard Niebuhr, Rudolf Bultmann, Karl Barth, and Emil

Brunner—I knew the whole bunch! We were on the World Council of Churches' Faith and Order Commission together. For thirty years of my life I was a member of the group I now sardonically remember called itself "the younger theologians." We met twice a year in the House of Preachers at Washington Cathedral, because it was offered to us and it was cheap. Other members of the group were Henry Pitney Van Dusen, James Luther Adams, Wilhelm Pauck, and Paul Tillich. Now Jim Adams and I are the only two left.

We respond with a combination of rejoicing and melancholy. One would think that to talk of aging in true and realistic terms of diminishment, of passingness, would be depressing to the aged. Take it from me, the very opposite is the case. When I appear among my peers—old people who ask me sometimes to come because they know my special interest in them—when I come and give them bits of the literature on aging, which I know by heart now and can recite to them, I find that they both weep and are consoled, because they know they are not alone. This is the human condition; this is the company toward membership in which we all are moving.

Heaven Is a Metaphor

Heaven is a metaphor for the fulfillment of life in God. I remember once I was interim pastor in a congregation and a lady came to me, a nice lady who had experienced a very fulfilling and wonderful marriage. Her husband had died the autumn before, and she was in deep grief. She said, "You know, it's particularly hard late in the afternoon sitting at the window watching where he used to come around the corner in summertime, his coat over his arm, slapping his leg with the evening paper. He always stopped just when he thought I couldn't see him and knocked out his pipe. He knew I didn't want him to smoke so much, although I kept sewing up the burnt holes in his coat pockets. That time of day is a terrible one for me to get through, because I know he won't come around the corner any more. In heaven do you suppose he and I will live together in a cottage with a white fence?"

This was pathetic. I appreciate the woman's grief and affection, but I can't say, "Yes, yes, in heaven that's the way it's going to be." That would be a lie. Who would manufacture the old shag tobacco in heaven? There would have to be a pipe-making shop and a tweed jacket to carry the pipe in. That is simply not true to the Christian faith.

We Must Stop

We must stop this conspiracy of silence about death, and talk openly about it. One can go to church a whole lifetime and never hear a sermon on death.

If I were a young preacher again, I would preach the Christian gospel of eternal life in God, but I would preach it sooner in my ministry, preach it throughout, and I would preach it more realistically. The Bible really has nothing to say about eternal life. That sounds like a shocking statement, but it's literally true: there is not a single clear and concrete word in the Bible about life after death. It affirms that life with God is life with that which does not die. But any specification about life after death is steadily avoided by the biblical writers.

Paul made an effort to address the question, but it's a bum effort: "What you sow does not come to life unless it dies. And what you sow is not the body which is to be, but a bare kernel, perhaps of wheat or of some other grain. But God gives it a body as he has chosen, and to each kind of seed its own body. For not all flesh is alike, but there is one kind for men, another for animals, another for birds, and another for fish" (1 Cor. 15:36-39). He tries by natural analogy to say something. Interestingly, he never tried it again.

In Romans

In Romans, the most mature of Paul's epistles, he says, "If we live, we live to the Lord, and if we die, we die to the Lord; so then, whether we live or whether we die, we are the Lord's" (Rom. 14:8). Period! That is the fundamental and absolute word of Scripture. But that word is immensely satisfying to old people. I never try to give any blueprints of eternity or heaven or eternal life, since by definition it is utterly impossible.

By Faith

I think instead of trying to answer all the questions about death, we ought to follow the example of Paul and the New Testament and say, "Eye has not seen nor ear heard"; "By faith we are saved."

By faith we are saved.

Questions for Discussion

1. What does it mean to go grow old in a culture that is obsessed by youth? Why are we told that aging is something to be avoided or at least delayed? In what ways do we unconsciously accept this belief?

2. Sittler writes that aging and death define the limits of methodological models and managerial powers (p. 70). How has our desire to solve this "awkward problem" led to a devaluation of human life?

3. How does Sittler's definition of "pathos" (p. 70) give the word "pathetic" a new sense of philosophical significance and depth of meaning?

4. Rather than search for a solution to "the human condition for which there is no solution" (p. 71), how does Sittler suggest we encounter aging? Why is that movement so difficult for us?

5. Read the section "We Must Stop" (p. 74). When a seed is sown, it does not grow—becoming a larger seed. It breaks open, changes, and sends out root and shoot. Reflect on transition and change in aging, death, and the promise of eternal life.

6. What is your response to the woman's question in "Heaven Is a Metaphor" (pp. 73-74)? What response answers her "pathetic" question yet is true to the Christian faith (see question 3 above)?

7. Sittler encourages us to join his journey "for courage, acquiescence, resignation, acceptance—some coming to terms with" (p. 71). In what ways is this journey the roadmap for this whole book? Is this journey "up theology" (a human endeavor to reach God) or is it "down theology" (God reaching to humanity)? Explore your responses.

8. How is Sittler's encouragement "to a graceful-letting be" (p. 71) a corollary to St. Paul's "For by grace you have been saved through faith, and this is not your own doing; it is the gift of God" (Ephesians 2:8) and ""What no eye has seen, nor ear heard, nor the human heart conceived, what God has prepared for those who love him" (1 Corinthians 2:9)?

Other Lutheran Voices Titles

Reclaiming the "L" Word by Kelly A. Fryer
96 pages, 0-8066-4596-2

Reclaiming the "L" Word is a book about renewing congregations by recognizing and living out the core teachings of the Lutheran faith.

Getting Ready for the New Life by Richard F. Bansemer
96 pages, 0-8066-4988-7

The book consists of fifteen devotional readings followed by Scriptural texts, prayers, and reflection questions. Intended for use by those facing suffering and loss, those who provide them with comfort and care, and groups wanting to explore and share their experiences.

Listen! God Is Calling! by D. Michael Bennethum
96 pages, 0-8066-4991-7

Presents Martin Luther's teaching on vocation as a resource both for individual believers, helping them find deeper meaning in their ordinary daily labors; and for congregations, encouraging them to develop a climate that supports their members at work.

On a Wing and a Prayer by Michael L. Cooper-White
96 pages, 0-8066-4992-5

Uses the language of aviation to look at the principles of leadership and apply them to congregations and other organizations. Concepts such as visioning, strategic planning, calculated risk-taking, flexibility, and discovering the gifts of others are included.

Available wherever books are sold.

Other Lutheran Voices Titles

Give Us This Day by Craig L. Nessan
96 pages, 0-8066-4993-3

The Lord's Prayer demonstrates how justice for the
hungry is also deeply rooted in the teaching of Jesus.
The author summons the Christian church to listen
to the cries of the hungry and commit itself to ending
hunger as a matter of status confessionis.

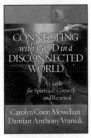

Connecting with God in a Disconnected World
by Carolyn Coon Mowchan and Damian Anthony Vraniak
96 pages, 0-8066-4996-8

Designed to encourage adult readers to explore and examine
the barriers that sometimes keep us from experiencing a
closer and more full relationship with God in Christ, and
our relationships in faith with one another.

Signs of Belonging by Mary E. Hinkle
96 pages, 0-8066-4997-6

Explores Luther's teaching on the seven marks of the
church: possession of the Word, Baptism, Sacrament of the
Altar, Office of the Keys, Office of Ministry, Discipleship,
and the cross (suffering on account of one's faith).

Will I Sing Again? by John McCullough Bade
96 pages, 0-8066-4998-4

Author John McCullough Bade reflects on his personal
struggle with Parkinson's Disease. Through narrative and
poetic passages, he searches for signs of God's grace in
the midst of his physical struggle and sense of loss.

Available wherever books are sold.

Other Lutheran Voices Titles

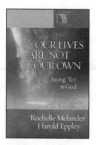

Our Lives Are Not Our Own
by Rochelle Melander and Harold Eppley
96 pages, 0-8066-4999-2

Designed to encourage personal reflection and create dialogue about Christian accountability. God calls us to the blessing of accountability, not the burden.

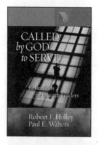

Open the Doors and See All the People
by Norma Cook Everist
112 pages, 0-8066-5161-X

Emerging from the author's interviews and interactions with numerous Lutheran congregations across the country, this book explores how congregations are determining and living out their identity.

Called by God to Serve
by Robert F. Holley and Paul E. Walters
96 pages, 0-8066-5172-5

Church councils and leadership groups will discover ten helpful devotional reflections and discussion starters for a three-year cycle, focusing on the task of serving from a biblical and theological perspective.

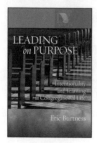

Leading on Purpose by Eric Burtness
96 pages, 0-8066-5174-1

Exploring the Purpose-Driven Church phenomenon, Eric Burtness provides pastors and church leaders with a Lutheran view of what it means to lead on purpose and integrates the Purpose-Driven philosophy into the context of Lutheran congregational life.

Available wherever books are sold.